TAKE HER, SHE'S YOURS

BEFORE YOU START TO READ THIS BOOK, take this moment to think about making a donation to punctum books, an independent non-profit press,

@ https://punctumbooks.com/support/

If you're reading the e-book, you can click on the image below to go directly to our donations site. Any amount, no matter the size, is appreciated and will help us to keep our ship of fools afloat. Contributions from dedicated readers will also help us to keep our commons open and to cultivate new work that can't find a welcoming port elsewhere. Our adventure is not possible without your support.

Vive la Open Access.

Fig. 1. Hieronymus Bosch, *Ship of Fools* (1490–1500)

TAKE HER, SHE'S YOURS. Copyright © 2020 by Eva-Lynn Jagoe. This work carries a Creative Commons BY-NC-SA 4.0 International license, which means that you are free to copy and redistribute the material in any medium or format, and you may also remix, transform and build upon the material, as long as you clearly attribute the work to the authors (but not in a way that suggests the authors or punctum books endorses you and your work), you do not use this work for commercial gain in any form whatsoever, and that for any remixing and transformation, you distribute your rebuild under the same license. http://creativecommons.org/licenses/by-nc-sa/4.0/

First published in 2020 by punctum books, Earth, Milky Way.
https://punctumbooks.com

ISBN-13: 978-1-950192-81-6 (print)
ISBN-13: 978-1-950192-82-3 (ePDF)

DOI: 10.21983/P3.0290.1.00

LCCN: 2020936284
Library of Congress Cataloging Data is available from the Library of Congress

Book design: Vincent W.J. van Gerven Oei
Cover image: Remedios Varo, *Mujer Saliendo del Psicoanalista (Podría ser Juliana)*, 1960. Oil on canvas. Courtesy of Banco de Imágenes de VEGAP.

HIC SVNT MONSTRA

Eva-Lynn Jagoe

Take Her, She's Yours

p.

Contents

Prologue   15

PART ONE   19
*Phone Number · Fishing · In Thrall · La americana · Trying Not To
Understand · Ocean · Two Doctors · Take Her · Shortcut · Virgin Mary ·
Where the Couch Was · Selkie · Ooze · Native Skin · Umbrella · Daddy
Issues · Self-Fashioning · Nobody · Women's World · Fridays · "What Does a
Woman Want?" · Entrapment · Splitting · Deserving*

PART TWO   99
*Catch Me · De Man · Holding · Monogamy · Porous · Its Own World · Too
Much · Into the Destructive Element · Not Knowing · Cockroaches · The
One · Cuckoo · Leda and the Swan · Animation · Error · L'inutile beauté ·
Dora and the Door · Run, Run, Run If You Can*

PART THREE   151
*Rats · At the Beginning · Blanking Out · The Dwarves · Drift · How the
Mighty Are Fallen · My Other Half · Ever After · Bloodlines · Leave ·
Anti-Revelation · Hot Water Bottle · July Weekend · You Fucked Up My Life ·
Heartbeat · The Third Term · One More Twist in the Spiral · Hue · Five
Years In · Personal Writing · Georgian Bay · End of Analysis*

Endnotes   205

Bibliography   209

Acknowledgments

I am grateful to my institutional homes, the Centre for Comparative Literature and the Spanish and Portuguese Department at University of Toronto, for providing me the space, the freedom, and the encouragement to write what I've needed to write. In this generous setting, I have been able to teach my seminar, "Forms of Critical Writing," multiple times. To all of you brave students, thank you for making a space with me in which we could risk exposure and failure in order to experiment with our ideas and words. The Jackman Humanities Institute generously supported an earlier iteration of this project. I am so grateful to Vincent W.J. van Gerven Oei and Eileen A. Fradenburg Joy of punctum books for their vision, their knowledge, and their support in bringing this book into the world. A special thanks to Vincent, for your assiduous editorial work during the difficult first weeks of the coronavirus pandemic.

Irina Sadovina said, after reading this book, "it is not always easy to be confronted by the disturbing and implicating ways that another person unconsciously organizes herself." To the incredible people who have been willing to be confronted, and to give me feedback, thank you, you have made this a better book: Irina, Lauren Kirshner, Amira Mittermaier, Alex Marzano-Lesnevitch, Said Sayrafiezadeh, Chloe Higgins, Manjula Stokes, Shanna MacNair and Scott Wolven of The Writer's Hotel, Valentina Napolitano, Katie Lew, and Catherine Fatima. And thank you to all the perceptive friends and family who've asked the serious questions that I need to be able to answer, in life and in writing: Lisa Moore, Lauren Berlant, Claudia Rankine, Amy De'Ath, Maria Jagoe, Georgy Kronfeld, Maddie Kronfeld, Dima Kronfeld, Eric Cazdyn, Victoria McKenzie, Camilla Gibb, Al

Moritz, Gretchen Bakke, and Viviane Weitzner. Eve Sedgwick's teaching, talking, and writing resonate through these pages in ways that I didn't recognize for years. I wish we could talk together about this book.

Elspeth Brown and Catherine Taylor and Dalia Kandiyoti, your friendship and honest words have been touchstones for me, again and again. You sustain and nourish my thoughts and my days.

Alicia Naranjo, gracias por esa noche en la cocina, y tantas otras charlas a través de los años. Jay and Eva Jagoe, I am so happy that we've had all these years to know each other in the intimate ways that transcend the parent–daughter relationship portrayed here. Your stories touch me and fill me with wonder at all the different selves you have been in your lives. Lolita, te llevo dentro de mí, con agradecimiento y amor.

One day last year I went to a talk at University of Toronto. Sitting across the room from me was a man who looked familiar. I thought, with a jolt, that it was David's shrink, a man I'd only met once. How strange to be sitting across from a man who knew so much about my ex's psyche! I tried not to stare. About five minutes into the talk, I was flooded with the flustered, amused, and confused realization that it wasn't David's shrink, it was *mine*. Dr. O, even though you were so present to me as I wrote this book, I didn't recognize you. I hope, however, that you'll recognize us in these pages.

David Thomson, when I first told you I'd written a book in which the narrator is married to someone named David, I asked you if I should change the name. You said, "Nah, take it, I should get around to changing it anyway." I'm glad that you didn't, and honoured that you have given this book your blessing. You live in these pages in a version that is not yours, but that is, as you say, a "good-enough" one.

Imre Szeman, you were by my side all those days when I would get stuck, or filled with doubt, or couldn't stop crying. I know some of this book causes you pain, which makes me even more grateful for your support, your love, and your constant encouragement. Thank you for the gorgeous space of our days, for the joyful adventures, and for the plenitude of our lives together.

Sebastian and Liam, I don't need you to ever read this book, but I hope that if you do, its story will come at a time that will help you hold your own many selves. My love for you made telling this story so necessary, and so hard. I dedicate this book to you.

PROLOGUE

By the time she had grown sharper, she found in her mind a collection of images and echoes to which meanings were attachable — images and echoes kept for her in the childish dusk, the dim closet, the high drawers, like games she wasn't yet big enough to play.

— Henry James, *What Maisie Knew*

"I told my therapist about you and the dresser."

Se me encoge el corazón, Dolores used to say as she bandaged my gouged knee or bleeding elbow: *my heart is shrinking in on itself.*

That's what I feel when Sebastian reminds me of that frantic time four years earlier, when we were moving, yet again. The big lumbering dresser had been in my life since grad school, when I found it at a secondhand store. I hand-painted it with scenes of mountain climbers. Behind one of the handles, I hid a heart with "D+E" in the middle. After his dad and I divorced, Sebastian used it. The top right drawer was for his special stuff: photos, Grandpa's watch, a troll doll, a jar of weed, five dollars in coins he and his friend had watched someone drop under their car and quietly collected when he left. When the junk guys came, I let them cart it away without checking if the drawers were empty.

When he sees me cringe, Sebastian says, "It's okay, Mom."

"No, Seb, it's not." I don't want him to absolve me, though I probably begged for his forgiveness when he got home from school that day. Or, worse — my heart recoils again — I may have blamed him for not packing up his room in anticipation of the move. I don't remember. I don't want to know if he does.

David, reading these pages, says, "Tell your readers that your ex says that you were a really good mom." So there you go, it's been said, but it's not what I'm going to write about in these pages. Because open-hearted love — the mornings when Seb comes home from university and I wake him by stroking his pale shoulder as he smiles into the dog's licking face, and then Liam rushes in, jumping on top of his brother and kissing loudly into his ear, all shrieks and laughter and me tickling whatever entangled long limb flashes past me as they wrestle — these quotidian intimacies don't make for a good story.

Instead, this is a very personal story about how I learned, well, *to not take myself so personally*. The learning involved a lot of fear and rage and sticky mess, because it turned out that I was really invested in the idea of who I was. It took years for me to begin to accept that I knew so little of what compelled me to act and think and be the way I was. Like Henry James's Maisie, I have, over this process, "grown sharper." This book explores the meanings that I have come to attach to the "collection of images and echoes" that linger in my mind.

I don't want to undo the fact that I threw that dresser away. That's way too important in both of our psyches. But I wish Sebastian and I could peer down into that high drawer together. I imagine him picking up his chess competition ribbon or a Lego figurine, and telling me what it means to him. I listen. Then I tell him what it makes me think of. Each of us invests the contents of the drawer with stories that are particular to our own histories and knowledges. The next day, maybe he tells me something else, even if it contradicts or confuses his story from the day before. Perhaps that leads me to change my story.

The dialogue that I imagine, in which we try out stories, not holding each other to any definitive version, is what I now think of as intimacy. This intimacy is one in which we are not fully in control of who we are or what we do, and that is okay. Neither of us holds ourselves or the other to account for these incoherencies. Our relationship has enough deep drawers that it can hold all the junk, vital and treasured, of our selves.

PART ONE

Therein lies the problem with self-help books: selves are not that easy to help. An individual requires a kind of nurturing and growth that goes far beyond aerobics and quick-fix therapy.

— Jonathan Lear, *Love and Its Place in Nature*

PART ONE

Phone Number

I got Dr. O's number from Professor C. Professor C would become my husband's shrink. Dr. O would become mine. My husband would become my ex. There was a lot of becoming to come in the next five years, but I didn't know that as I wrote down Dr. O's phone number.

Professor C was in academic mode when I met him at a conference. As we chatted about the state of Comparative Literature today, he mentioned that he was also a practicing psychoanalyst. I had read a lot of psychoanalytic theory, but had never met an analyst in the flesh. I was full of questions, but he politely deflected them, guiding the conversation towards the panel we had just attended. Neither of us, it seemed, was interested in the other's conversational gambits.

At the end of the conference, I couldn't resist asking, in a deliberately casual manner, whether he was taking new patients. He was, on weekends. That wouldn't work for me, since I didn't want to give up time with my kids to go to an analyst. I asked if he knew of anyone else, and he suggested Dr. O, a colleague of his at the Toronto Psychoanalytic Society and a member of the Lacan study group.

I was looking for a new kind of therapy. For two years, I had been going to weekly therapy with a sweet, attentive woman named Wendy. We met in her slightly dated condo that looked out over a leafy Toronto ravine. The marble entryway and the overly attentive concierge reminded me of the place my parents bought after they sold my childhood home.

Wendy dressed in silky blouses and soft knit cardigans, her curly salt and pepper hair casually piled on top of her head. I loved her tiny frame, her throaty laugh, the quizzical turn of her head that urged me to explain myself. I was pretty sure she reciprocated my affection, though I told myself not to believe it, that it was just what being in therapy was. But she sometimes wiped tears from her eyes when I recounted a particularly heart-wrenching memory. Watching the emotions play across her face elicited pity in me for the child I once was.

At first, it felt like a gift. She provided a safe space for me to feel anger or sadness. During our sessions, she gazed earnestly at me from the bottom of an overstuffed armchair. If I was self-critical, she begged me not to be hard on myself, telling me that I was brave and accomplished. Once, I told her that George Eliot's novel, *Daniel Deronda,* was a touchstone for me. Each time I read it, I identified with a different character or situation. Over the next month, she tried to read it, and was embarrassed that she couldn't get through it. I also was embarrassed that I had made her feel intellectually inferior by talking about a book that she found inaccessible. I reassured her that her wisdom and advice were exactly what I needed.

When I called her, sobbing, to say that I had kissed a former lover at work, she made time for me immediately. I walked in panicked. What was wrong with me? Why wasn't I content to be back together with David? Had I just fucked everything up? She reassured me that no harm was done, and that I could, with her help, avoid repeating this transgression. She suggested that I start coming twice a week, and for ninety instead of fifty minutes. I was so grateful that she was willing to support me.

Over the next year, I'd burst into the door, so eager to launch into our conversations that I didn't notice the whiff of cigarette smoke that hung over the hallway. She was getting even skinnier. Sometimes when she talked, a cough burst through thick-sounding phlegm and rattled her whole body. I ignored it. It wasn't any of my business, and I didn't want to come across as nosy.

It must have been hard for her to break the news to me. Her lung cancer was back. She didn't have long. I could ask her anything.

What about me? was what I wanted to wail. Instead I quietly asked if she smoked. She told me she had started as a teen. When she first got diagnosed, she quit. Now that it was back, there was no reason to resist her addiction, so she was back to heavy smoking. I hid my disapproval, and began to cry.

She cried too. Later that evening, she wrote me an email: "I have referred all my other clients to a colleague, but I don't want to leave you. Any contact with you — for me — is better than none. If you want, I will continue to see you as long as I am able."

"I'll take every moment I can get," I responded.

It didn't last long. Sick from all the medication, she called to cancel a session at the last minute. She could barely get the words out through the hacking cough. I had just come out of the subway, so I stumbled around the supermarket nearby, unsure what to do with the empty hour stretching out in front of me. I bought her a potted pink azalea that reminded me of my childhood in the lush suburbs of Washington, DC, and left it with her concierge.

She emailed, "I think of you, as I have so often said, so very often and the flowers will be a treasured way of doing so. (Wish so deeply that I could do so much more than that)."

What more did she wish she could do? It had always been like this with us — her worrying about me, me feeling like I didn't quite understand who she thought I was. I felt like I was trying to want for myself what I thought she wanted me to want.

When she died, I was bereft. How was I going to control my impulses without her to guide me and reassure me? Talking to her had made me aware how little I understood my own actions.

I was also angry. She had blurred the lines so much that I felt responsible for her emotions. It was hard to disentangle what I needed from what she expected me to need, which was her, at any cost. Wendy hadn't been able to let me go.

A month after her death, I knew I wanted to continue therapy. It had to be different though. The therapist mustn't be my confidante or my friend. I hoped that the parameters of formal psychoanalysis might guard against the kind of slippage that I had experienced with Wendy. In May 2009, I called Dr. O. The voice I heard on the answering machine was deep and hoarse, with a whisper and crackle to it. He was either a very serious and stern man, or his vocal chords were damaged. *Not another smoker!* I thought.

I left a perky and professional message. His return call came at ten minutes to the hour. He explained that two initial consultations were required before he could decide whether or not to take on the analysis. Then he gave me the address along with specific directions: I was to walk up the driveway along the side of his house, open the door, descend the five steps to the basement. I should take care, if I was tall, to duck my head because the ceiling was low. I would enter into a waiting room that had a bathroom in case I needed it. I found his directions overly solicitous, so I just wrote down his address in my agenda.

The day of our appointment, I came out of the subway into a wealthy area of Toronto that I had never had any reason to visit before. The houses were bigger, the shops more upscale than where I lived. Adjacent to the subway was a small playground, filled with a cluster of Filipina nannies and their blond charges. Tagalog has many loanwords from Spanish, my mother tongue, so I understood them to be complaining about their employers and swapping news about their families back home. The children shrieked and slid while the babies stared passively out from their strollers.

When I arrived at the large detached house, I admired the tended front garden and tried to avert my eyes from peeking through the sheer curtains hanging in the living room window. After Wendy, I didn't want to know anything about a therapist's private life. I opened the side door and saw a pair of large black sneakers in the boot tray next to the door. Maybe I was supposed to take my shoes off too, but I was wearing sandals, and there was no way I was going to walk into his office barefoot. As I descended the steps, I hit my head on the low ceiling.

There was a sign on a closed door that said "Please Do Not Knock." The door to the bathroom was ajar. I sat on a small upholstered chair next to the radio, which was playing bombastic classical music. On the wall opposite me was a bookshelf of psychotherapy books from the 1970s and '80s. There was no Freud or any of the psychoanalytic theorists, despite what I knew about Dr. O from an internet search: that he was engaged in ongoing study of Freud, Jacques Lacan, D.W. Winnicott, and Wilfred Bion.

The door opened, and a heavyset bald man still wearing his workplace identification badge shuffled out, looking sad and preoccupied. Definitely the wearer of those tired shoes. I quickly averted my gaze as he squeezed past me to go to the bathroom.

A slim middle-aged man, wearing a button-down shirt and a knit vest, came to the door and, gravelly-voiced, said, "Ms. Jagoe? Please come in."

I picked up my backpack and walked in, closing the door behind me as Dr O. sat at a desk, swiveling his chair to face a small sofa. He gestured towards it. I smiled so as to show my comfortable and fearless attitude. He didn't smile back.

An interrogation began. He asked me questions from a sheet in front of him, and scribbled down the answers. The topics were less about my present circumstances than about earliest memories, youthful romantic attachments, and other therapy experiences. I liked the way his questions made me remember things that weren't usually part of the stories I told about my childhood.

The next visit I came ready to talk about the love letters I had written to the boy next door when I was thirteen. It was quickly clear, however, that I wasn't setting the agenda. Dr. O launched in by asking about my family structure, focusing particularly on Dolores, the Salvadorean housekeeper who had been my primary caregiver. I started to cry when I talked about how I had bounced back and forth between Dolores and my mother, trying to get from one what I couldn't get from the other.

Without acknowledging my tears, he said, "Double life…."

"Hmm," I said knowingly, and then immediately wished I hadn't pretended to understand.

At the end, Dr. O looked me in the face and told me he would enter into an analysis with me, which meant a commitment of four days a week. Since he was an MD, those sessions would be covered by Ontario health insurance, but if I missed a day I had to pay since he couldn't charge insurance for that session.

What I really wanted to ask was how many months or years the analysis would take. I knew that there was a Freud essay entitled "Analysis, Terminal and Interminable," which didn't sound good to me. Either it kills you or it never ends? I wanted some promise of closure, of cure. I wanted it in as efficient and efficacious manner as possible. Always quick at getting tasks done, I hoped that in this scenario I would also be speedier than most. I was at least bound to be smarter than that middle-management guy whose session had preceded mine, I figured.

I didn't, however, ask Dr. O what time frame I was committing to. I felt a dogged determination to not demonstrate doubt. I just said, "Yes, I'll start."

He said, "Don't you want to go home and talk it over with your husband?"

I bristled that he assumed I needed David's permission and was about to wave away his concern when he said, "Analysis is a big commitment and it will affect your family's schedules and trips. They should be consulted before you commit."

So he wasn't alluding to a husband's authority. He was telling me something that I didn't quite get about how what I did impacted others. I wasn't ready to think about that yet. I just responded, "No, it'll be fine, I know I can fit it into my schedule."

I got my agenda out and we agreed upon a time.

As I wrote it down, I said, "I'll call you if it turns out that the time doesn't work for me. What's your number?"

Silence. I glanced up and saw him looking straight at me. Had he not heard me?

Not a good sign for someone who was supposedly trained to be a good listener!

I repeated, "Your phone number?"

With his chin resting on his hand, he said, "Why don't we see where that phone number could be? The analysis has begun."

Fishing

Walking home, I caught a glimpse of my sons' messy hair and skinny legs racing by as I took the shortcut home from the subway. They were playing with the kids who lived in the apartment rental towers across the street from our house.

"Be home in an hour for dinner!" I called out to them, nodding to the Tibetan, Caribbean, and Pakistani grandmothers chatting on the benches. Those women probably had already made meals that their adult children would eat when they came home from work. I imagined trying to explain to them that I had just agreed to do psychoanalysis. It seemed so time-consuming and self-absorbed. I realized there was no way I was going to tell my parents. My Spanish mother would say I was just like those neurotic housewives she couldn't stand, wanting to talk endlessly about their problems and their sex lives. "It's always the mother's fault anyway," she often said. "That's what it comes down to with psychiatrists, no? The mother?"

When I called out to say I was home, David answered from the roof, "Climb out the window and come up here! I've been doing yoga in the sun. It's beautiful!"

I peered up from the stairwell to the hole in the ceiling. His plan was to build a turreted skylight using some window panes he'd found in a dumpster. It had been a month since he sawed the slightly crooked rectangle, but it was still an open hole that needed to be covered with a tarp. He poked his head, haloed by sunlit curls, through the hole, looking both delighted and sheepish that he hadn't been working on the construction. I rolled my eyes at his grin.

"No, I'm not coming up there," I said. It scared me to climb through the window and stand on the tilting roof. Plus I had to make dinner.

He was in a buoyant mood, and said, "Hey, whadya think of the shrink? Shrinky-dink? Gonna shrink my dink?"

I said, "It's already shrinking from your bad jokes!"

I went back downstairs, picking up shoes, dirty laundry, and Legos on my way. The kitchen counter was piled up with the breakfast dishes and David's papers and books. I knew that he would justify not having cleaned up by saying that a sunny day shouldn't be wasted by being cooped up inside. I agreed, in principle, but still felt resentful.

All three of them hated the meal. I said, "Come on, it's good to try something different!"

I don't like cod either. I didn't tell them that I had bought it after leaving Dr. O's office. I was so ashamed that I'd been caught out asking for something I didn't need: the phone number of a man I had called in the first place. I'd walked out of his basement and stumbled into a fishmonger's down the street. In a flirty way, I asked the elderly Portuguese merchant for advice, even though I was grossed out at his condescending macho manner towards me. So when he suggested the cod, I smiled and bought it, even though I knew we all preferred salmon.

After dinner, while Sebastian and Liam chased each other around the house with swords, David did the dishes. This time, it was me that felt sheepish. I wrapped my arms around him from behind and breathed in the warm smell of his back, saying, "Um, how would you feel if I told you that I agreed to enter into analysis with Dr. O?"

I was getting ready to explain why I wanted to do it, but David just turned around and said, "I want to do it too."

How did he always manage to turn conversations around so they were about him? I moved to the other side of the counter. "But we can't both! What about the kids and the dog and everything? It's already going to be so time-consuming with me having four sessions a week. I'm going to need to stay at the university late some nights to just catch up on everything."

Then I remembered Professor C. "You could do it on weekends! It's not like we have such a great time on weekends anyway."

We both grimaced, remembering last weekend's fight. The neighbor got mad at David for climbing his tree, and I got mad that he'd embarrassed us. We had yelled at each other in front of the boys. I said, "Maybe it'll be good for you to have something to do while I'm hanging out with the kids. I think you could get him to charge you on a sliding scale."

David hadn't had a job in years, so I was worried about our ever-increasing debt. And I hadn't even asked Dr. O how much he was going to charge me for missed sessions. But it would be unfair if I just went ahead and did it. I felt like I had to give David the opportunity if he wanted it. It could be good for our family. Maybe a shrink would help him to understand why he had so much trouble finishing his book project. Or why he couldn't keep a job as a professor or even a lecturer. If so, it would be worth the money.

The closer the Monday came to start the analysis, the more panicked I felt. That weekend, I had anxiety dreams. In one, I was five minutes late for analysis and Dr. O had two other men in the room. When I tried to go in, he said, "We're having a consultation, please wait."

He closed the door, and the hour went by before he opened it again. I marched in and sat on his lap, saying in a faux pouty way, "You didn't give me my time!"

He responded gruffly by mimicking me, "Give me attention! Love me! Get it up!"

I woke with the same self-conscious feeling I'd had when he hadn't given me his number. What if I spent my sessions constantly trying to arouse his interest? What if I turned out to be the cock tease he accused me of being in the dream?

In Thrall

Dr. O opened the door for me that Monday, and I walked over to the small sofa on which I'd sat for the consultations. Then I looked at the chaise longue that stood against the back wall. I had seen out of the corner of my eye the week before, but hadn't really acknowledged it. That would have been like inspecting the operating table while talking to a surgeon about an impending procedure.

This time, he gestured towards it. Without a word, I quickly lay on it, smoothing my skirt and crossing my legs. It felt like a movie, me lying on the couch with him behind my head. I heard him rustling papers, clearing his throat. The leather chair that he was sitting in creaked as he shifted his weight. I recrossed my legs and folded my hands over my abdomen. Peering around the room, I glanced at the wall-to-wall neutral carpeting. Laying over top of it was a woven Latin American wool rug with a wrinkle in the middle that I wanted to pull flat. The window wells held carved wooden objects or polished stones. The painting in front of me was an abstract and unobtrusive red and orange. When the air conditioning kicked off, I heard him breathing behind me. We were alone. The focus was on what I was going to say next.

"I feel so stupid," I started. "Spoiled. About the phone number. Like you caught me out trying to get you to give me something."

After a long pause, in which I wondered if I was supposed to keep talking or if he was listening, Dr. O said, "Maybe you didn't need my number on a logistical level. But on an emotional level perhaps you were asking me whether I will give you the help you feel you need."

This seemed less judgmental than I had imagined him to be. He wasn't acting like the shaming doctor of my dream.

That first week, I didn't talk about anything that I would have expected. Instead, I told him a seemingly random story that my sister had told me about her friend X. X had been sexually abused as a girl by her father and brothers on the Virgin Islands until she went to the States to live with her mother and stepfather. As she entered puberty, the stepfather suggested that, because she was sexually traumatized, X was in danger of being preyed upon and making bad decisions for herself. He offered himself as her lover who could teach her consensual sex. She and her mother agreed. X and her stepfather had sex until she was of marrying age. Her future husband was apprised of the situation and enlisted to care for her. Twenty years later, she and her husband continued to think of the stepfather as an exceptionally progressive paternal figure.

I could barely get the story out. My breathing was jagged. I clenched my jaw to keep it from shaking. Tears rolled down the corners of my eyes as I said, "I imagine her, lying in the dark, the air all tropical around her. She's listening for footsteps. Scared to go to sleep because one of the men in the household is sure to come into her room. Maybe one of them acts like her ally, even as he rapes her."

I pictured the suburban American bedroom that had been her refuge from that violent island house. There, too, she would have waited for a man who was going to have sex with her. This time, though, it was couched as part of her education and care. "He probably taught her to ask for what she wanted. As if she would know. How *could* she know her own sexual desire, with that amount of trauma?"

Dr. O echoed my question with a murmured, "How could she know what she wanted?"

"It's an incest story with a twist," I said. "The stepfather and the mother pride themselves on being free of cultural taboos. The girl is taught to be grateful that they are acting in her best interest."

This was how X had explained it. My sister and I talked for hours about how deluded the parents were if they seriously thought they were enlightened or progressive.

I didn't know why I had brought up this story when I didn't even know X. I was agitated, there in the dimly lit basement with a man I had recently met. Dr. O paused and then said, "What a tale of enthrallment and deception."

Upon hearing the word "enthrallment," I mumbled, "Thrall.... Thrill."

My word musing made me aware of the spine-shivering thrill of the story. I was horrified and fascinated by the girl's lack of agency. She was handed around like chattel, from one man to the next, each of them fucking her while pretending to care for her.

I said, "Wait, who was in thrall to whom? That whole wise and knowing man role that the stepfather played — I bet it masked something darker. He was probably turned on by her young body. By her being his wife's daughter."

I talked quietly, with long pauses in between as I let myself imagine the scenes of their encounters. "He'd fantasize about the next time, planning what he was going to do with her. He'd explain it to her in a fatherly tone. She was so malleable. He probably got off on his role as her protector and savior. She must have made him feel so powerful when she told him about how bad her life had been. He was enthralled."

I stopped, disgusted by what I had said. Dr. O said, "Are you asking me about what we will do in this room?"

That stopped me in my tracks. Was I? I had no idea why I was saying what I was saying. After a long pause, I said, "My hungover British uncle used to wink at me and say "the hair of the dog that bit me" as he poured himself a beer with his breakfast. Are you going to be the therapeutic "hair"? If I tell you about my fucked-up relationships with men, will you say we have to work through it by recreating my traumatic experiences in a controlled environment? Offer to cure me through a little more of the same? Will you say it's for my own good?"

My heart was racing. I waited for him to reassure me. To deny that he would ever do anything like that. I heard his pen scratch his notebook. He shifted in his chair.

I lay there, wondering if he was looking down the length of my body. Shrinks fucked their patients sometimes. They abused their power over the woman who were in thrall to them. Or maybe they were in thrall to the women who shared their innermost thoughts with them.

"I don't want to be oracular," I said, "but I know it will happen. You will listen to my stories and you will be enthralled by me. Like every other man to whom I've told my secrets. It's how I seduce them. And it's how I'll seduce you."

La americana

That week, my sister was in Washington, visiting my parents. She had reprogrammed the remote, organized their medicines, updated my dad's computer. I was glad, because I hate doing that stuff. My task is usually to help my mother go through her closet. I hold up each article of clothing, and she tells me the story of when she bought it, and for what occasion she wore it. I ask, "But have you worn it in the last year?"

As her social life and her capacities diminish, we discard shoes and dresses that will never be worn again. Sometimes, with a Jaeger's suit or a Saks Jandel dress that she really loves, I take it, saying that I'll have the hem let out or the sleeves lengthened. It makes it easier for her to give it up, despite the fact that I'm eight inches taller than her and it's obvious I'll never fit her clothes. They hang in my closet for months until I finally take them to Goodwill.

My sister and I were talking on the phone, something we do very seldom. When one of us is in DC, though, we call each other, needing to complain to someone who understands what it's like to be there.

My father was out at one of his philanthropic events. I knew that my mother wouldn't have gone with him. Her fatigue and disinterest in meeting people is the complete opposite of his bonhomie. He is popular in Washington, from the soup kitchens where his Mississippi accent emerges as he serves inner city homeless men, to the high society charitable events that he organizes.

My sister said, "Mom and I were sitting in the kitchen last night. Kaia came in and drank out of her bowl. Mom said, '*Ay, típico!* Why do dogs always have to come in and slurp water so loudly right when we're talking? They just want to get our attention!'"

I cracked up. "Speaking of typical! How narcissistic can she be? Not everything everyone does revolves around her!"

My sister was organizing the family photo albums. As a young woman, I had pulled them out every time I brought a new boyfriend home, showing him me as a fat baby, a sweet little long-haired girl, and a Dorothy Hamill-haircut tomboy tween. I hoped, I guess, that those images would make him fall in love with me even more.

Since my birthday was in late October, my parties were often Halloween costume parties. When I was five, I wore a Spanish flamenco dancer outfit, red with white polka dots, complete with a paper mask of a toothy woman with heavy dark eyelids. My mother had bought it at a tourist shop in Barcelona when she went home. Flamenco has nothing to do with her family background or Catalan culture, but in my father's social circles she was known as Little Spanish Eva, so she must have felt the need to show her heritage iconically. I remember I couldn't see through the mask, but had fun clacking the castanets.

For my sixth birthday, I wore a George Washington costume that had been my brother's. My parents must have bought it at Mount Vernon when they took a Spanish relative sightseeing. It had blue satin breeches and a waistcoat, a white frilly shirt with a big collar and puffy sleeves, and a tricorner hat. Dolores curled my hair up on either side of my head, and dusted it with Johnson's baby powder.

I said to my sister, "I thought George Washington was one of our ancestors! I mean, our brother is named George, and Mom used to decorate the table with little hatchets and fake cherries on the president's birthday."

My mother had inherited the decorations from her mother-in-law, the social secretary at the Pentagon under Eisenhower.

Before she died, my grandmother, a documented Daughter of the American Revolution, trained Little Eva in the customs of Washington society.

My sister, an American history buff, said, "You know that's just a myth to teach children about honesty? That whole thing about the young George saying, 'I cannot tell a lie, Father. I was the one who chopped your cherry tree' — it's not true."

"That knowledge comes way too late for me," I said. "I think I've always felt like I wasn't a true American descendant of G.W. since I lied to Dad about cutting something down."

It was when I was little, younger even than the George Washington party. Dolores and I took a walk in the early spring, picking a sweet bouquet of crocuses and violets and snowdrops from the neighbors' lawn. I gave them to my father to place in front of the Virgin Mary bust in the dining room. He asked where I'd gotten them.

My English wasn't good. My father, a businessman in his mid-50s, spoke no Spanish. I pointed up the street and said the neighbors' name. I had, he said, to take the flowers back, because that was stealing. By schooling me, he was sending an indirect message to Dolores, who he would never criticize to her face. Instead, he often loudly acclaimed her, insisting that she come to the table so that our guests could applaud her cooking. His extravagant clapping and pounding the table made up for the fact that he couldn't talk to her.

Dolores was making dinner when I came in crying and told her. She wiped her hands on her apron and we trudged back up the hill to the neighbors' house, where we stood, indecisive, on the curb. Neither of us could bring herself to ring the doorbell. Finally, I flung the wilted flowers across their lawn.

"They probably wouldn't have even known who you were," my sister said. "The neighbors all thought you were Dolores's illegitimate daughter, with your big brown eyes and your Spanglish!"

When we hung up, I went and found the DVD of the old Super 8 home movies. I scrolled through almost two hours before I got to that George Washington costume. The camera points first at the carved pumpkins, and then pans up to the stairs, where I'm standing holding the banister, striking a manly pose with one blue-satined leg bent. My chin is up, my gaze is serious. As if I could prove to my father, standing behind the camera, that I really am his American child.

Trying Not To Understand

I didn't tell my sister about the psychoanalysis. She was, at that time, going in the opposite direction, reading self-help books that asserted that you could shape your subconscious by affirming positive thoughts. I wanted to say that, in Freudian terms, it was the unconscious. And that, according to psychoanalytic theory, the unconscious was pretty impervious to self-help injunctions to look on the bright side of life. I didn't, however, say anything. It would have been like the *Daniel Deronda* incident with Wendy, where I would have felt embarrassed at having belittled the enthusiasm of a woman I respected and loved. Plus, what did I know? Maybe affirmations could change your neural patterns, and I was just indulging in some anachronistic practice that had been proven ineffective.

My mother's response, if I'd told her that I was in analysis, would have been that it was "so American" of me to talk about myself with a stranger. Which is ironic, considering Lacan's attacks on what he calls "the American way of life."[1] In *Écrits*, he says that the "ego psychology" practiced in the United States manipulates the patients and represses the unconscious. When I saw that he called this "American," I double-underlined it. The stereotyped dichotomies between the go-getter, self-help American ethos versus the more fatalistic, less individualistic Spanish mentality, were so rigidly defined in my household that I was always eager to collect evidence of them elsewhere.

In the period between Wendy's death and starting sessions with Dr. O, I had read a bunch of Lacan. Actually, I had read a lot *about* Lacan and slogged through a few of his essays and seminars. My motivations were mixed. I had an idea that my next academic project was going to be a book about sound, and that knowing about the practice of psychoanalytic listening could be useful. My plan was to look at contemporary Latin American artists, filmmakers, and writers who seemed to be foregrounding sound in order to articulate the difficulties of communication in their political and cultural contexts. I wasn't sure what I meant by that, but I knew I wanted to write about the films of Lucrecia Martel, the Argentine director who hears the whole soundscapes of her movies and then begins to imagine the visuals and plot. Martel's films, in my view, get at what can and cannot be heard or understood, in political, emotional, and intimate ways. Her *The Holy Girl* is my favorite movie because it captures the confusion and potential of a teenage girl who is negotiating the different discourses of family, religion, sexuality, and friendship.

In thinking about my own research project, I wanted to echo Martel's insistence on listening by calling for a self-aware practice of formal and contextual listening. Critical listening, such as that practiced in psychoanalysis, could, I hoped, serve as a supplement to the visual bias of traditional critical reading practices.

I have to admit that I wasn't just reading psychoanalytic texts as a scholar, though. I was also picking through them as if they were self-help, as if I could figure out why my therapy with Wendy had failed. I underlined sentences in Lacan, or in Bruce Fink's books *on* Lacan, as if they were direct answers to my questions. The first chapter of Fink's *Fundamentals of Psychoanalytic Technique: A Lacanian Approach for Practitioners* is entitled "Listening and Hearing." Unlike the theoretical texts I'd been trying to read, this book is about the practice of psychoanalysis, and I read it cover to cover. I copied out this phrase of Lacan's, figuring it would be the central idea of my research project:

> I repeatedly tell my students: "Don't try to understand!"... May one of your ears become as deaf as the other one must

> be acute. And that is the one that you should lend to listen for sounds and phonemes, words, locutions, and sentences, not forgetting pauses, scansions, cuts, periods, and parallelisms.[2]

Don't try to understand! Yes, that was what I was after. In my research, I didn't want to jump immediately to an interpretation of a text or an idea, producing scholarly articles that proved my theoretical knowledge. I wanted to take some time to listen without knowing what I was listening to.

When I started analysis with Dr. O, I stopped reading about psychoanalysis. It felt inappropriate, like I would be pulling back the curtain on what he was doing. I didn't want to know anything about his techniques in case they relied on my ignorance of them to be effective. I wished I hadn't read the Fink book, and never mentioned to Dr. O that I had.

I also started to lose interest in the research project. It would have been a logical next step for me. I taught Latin American film classes, and I was a specialist on Argentine literature and culture. On a research trip to Mexico City I had met many cool artists who happened to do formally innovative things with sound. But it had no real argument. It felt like a sterile investigation in which I would "apply" theoretical ideas to texts, picking ones that fit into the template, discarding others.

I didn't know, yet, how much the analysis was going to make me lose my footing. How I wasn't going to be able to maintain any kind of academic impartiality or critical distance from theory. How what I thought of as my "work" ideas were going to become urgent questions I needed to answer in order to figure out how to live in the world.

Ocean

In the third week of analysis, I had the first of many dreams of an ocean at nighttime. I'm standing on the coast, looking out at the huge waves, getting ready to dive into the dark waters even though I know there's a dangerous current below the surface. The surf pounds the shore and I'm paralyzed with fear.

My breathing was shallow and quick as I told Dr. O.

He murmured, "Undercurrent?"

It was like we were both half asleep, focusing on connotations that were tangential, or even slightly surreal. I remembered that my uncle was in the dream. The hair-of-the-dog one. When I was a teenager, he introduced me to the "finer things" of adult life: Spanish wines, Scottish whiskies, Gauloises cigarettes, escargots, animal organs, *Lady Chatterley's Lover,* Evelyn Waugh's diaries, stories of sexual misadventures. He was insatiable in his appetites. In the dream, he jumps in and mocks me for not following him. I yell "No, *I* can't risk going in that ocean. As in, '*You* can, but I can't protect myself enough to not drown in it all.'"

Dr. O said, "Into the destructive element?"

I said, "He's brazen. He'll swim in unprotected waters. But me, there's something wrong with me, my reactions are overwrought. I'll drown in it all. The booze or poetry or sex wreak havoc on my gut, my head, and my heart. I'm too sensitive about everything.... I mean, no one else I know needs to lie on a couch every day and talk about their dreams!"

A couple of days later, I had another dream. It's nighttime again. Big rocks are silhouetted by the moonlight. The whitecaps shine as they emerge from the dark water. I'm not scared of the ocean. I am alone. It feels that I always will be, that the beach stretches out forever and I am the only person on it.

Dr O said, "Rocks?"

Why did he always focus on such random things? "Um, yes. There were rocks. Oh wait, I remember. It was on a Spanish beach on the coast of Mallorca. My extended family had taken me there on a family trip when I was a teenager. In real life I wasn't alone in the moonlight. I was with the pilot."

Over many sessions, more of the story emerged from my memory. I told and retold it, worrying a word, an image, a feeling. What follows is a distillation. In the actual process of analysis, it took me months to come to this version, which I still don't believe is the only way to understand the event. It includes many of the things that I learned, as I talked to Dr. O, about my sexuality and my family. So it's going to come across as much more "knowing" than it was when I struggled through it on the couch. Just know that getting to this level of narrative assurance is:

- The work of many days of circling, analyzing, rethinking, and rejecting; and
- A ruse, a fictionalized account, an attempt to come across as a narrator who has understood her history and learned a lesson that she can impart to you. These stories never finish, never become fully knowable. Many of my friends have been experiencing this with the recent #MeToo movement. Stories that we thought we understood about our sexual encounters and fucked-up interactions with men in power have once again reared their heads, become so much more structural and omnipresent than we understood them when we first shared them with each other in our 20s.

Anyway, here's my version for now. That nighttime beach scene had been building up over a period of days. My cousin's husband had brought me and their children on this visit to his sister and her husband, a commercial pilot. She was sick the whole time we were there, so her husband was the one that took us out on his powerful motorboat. While the kids drank too much Coke and got sunburnt, I'd found my way to the wheel, where he taught me to steer the helm of the gleaming white boat into beautiful swimming coves. As I snuck glances at the blonde and silver hairs on his chest, his Rolex and wedding band glinting in the sun, I was acutely aware of his gaze on my tanned belly.

Back in Barcelona my body was looked at with less admiring eyes from the women of my mother's family. I was foreign to them, the product of an American regimen of milk-drinking and over-feeding. They spoke in judgmental tones about my long legs, rounded hips, loose limbs. Just recently, my mother had started saying, "I don't know what you do to men!" Did she really not know? Where she saw fat and gangliness, men saw voluptuous willowiness.

I liked that men found me sexy. I was excited by the rituals of seduction and the attentiveness from adults who had until recently not noticed me. I did something to them. Like Little Red Riding Hood, I ignored the warnings of my admonishing mother, and thrilled to the pleasantries of the wolf who encouraged me to diverge from the path and enjoy the wild wood. Instead of seeing me as a child in need of control, the wolf saw me as a delicious being. When Little Red exclaims about those big eyes, ears, hands, and mouth, she knows that she's not talking to granny. The dangerous male beast promises that everything he has is turned out just for her — the better to see her, listen to her, hold her, and eat her up. Like her, I could never refuse someone's hunger for me.

At the restaurant that third night, the married pilot kept my glass filled with wine. He grazed my thigh with his hand under the table. As we finished our cortado coffees, he casually told everyone that he would give me a ride back on his motorcycle. I felt special. No one was going to hold me back, not the boy cousin who wanted a ride, not my cousin's husband, not the pilot's wife, at home with a migraine. Actually, the only one who tried to keep me from going off alone with him was the envious boy. No one else stood in the pilot's way.

When I snuck back into the hotel room a couple of hours later, my fourteen-year-old cousin was awake and asked me where I had been. We stood in the moonlight whispering. I told her that the pilot had taken me to the beach to see the full moon, and angled myself so that she couldn't see the scratches and dirt on my back.

Maybe I didn't tell my cousin because she was still a girl, and I didn't want her to know that her dashing uncle was a wily wolf. Or maybe because I didn't have the words for it, my Spanish hardly up to the task. When I think about it now, I say it in English: "He ate me out." It wasn't just that I didn't have the linguistic ability to say it; it was also that I couldn't map it on the spectrum of my sexual knowledge at the time. He hadn't taken off any of his clothes. There had been no penetration or ejaculation. I knew from my mother that men always want one thing, that their need is so uncontrollable that it is up to us women to protect ourselves. So was what happened on the beach something he had given me, or something he had taken? Was that something men wanted to do, or was it something that I had unknowingly elicited?

The pilot is not in the beach dreams. It's not that I've erased his presence out of denial. It's that he wasn't a companion or a lover or an ally or a foe. Being there with him meant that I was alone, alone with a secret. My secret: of having kissed back, of having given him my pussy to eat, of doing something that only a sexually desirous woman would do.

As I talked more about this incident to Dr. O, I wondered where the adults were. My relatives — who knew he was a womanizer, who were responsible for taking care of the children — let me go with him. Perhaps they didn't interfere because it would have been embarrassing to confront him with the implication that he was untrustworthy. He was our gracious host, after all. Easier to let us go, the American girl and the married Spanish pilot. Unlike my younger girl cousins, I was flirty with him. I seemed to be able to hold my own in the adult dinner conversation.

"I guess," I said to Dr. O, "that they figured I could be thrown to the wolf. Given away to someone who seemed to really want me."

Two Doctors

I was awarded tenure at University of Toronto soon after I started analysis. I told Dr. O.

"Congratulations are, I believe, in order," he said in his usual formal way.

I shrugged dismissively. I hadn't doubted I was going to get it. My book was published; I had a bunch of articles published in respected journals; my teaching evaluations were good; I've done plenty of administrative service.

It was a different side of me from the crying fearful one who lay on the couch most of the time. Breezy, confident, assertive. This was the persona that I had adopted early in my academic career, even before I had publications. It had been a way to deal with the charged power dynamics that shaped so many of my interactions as a student and aspiring professor. The older male professors who liked their young female students to admire and look up to them, particularly appreciated it when the girls were smart and high-achieving. I guess it made them feel more relevant and valuable. I don't think I knew this consciously, but I certainly figured it out and carried it through my undergraduate and graduate life.

I didn't want Dr. O's congratulations for something that I already knew I did well. Though on the other hand, if he hadn't said something, I would have ascribed all kinds of weirdness to his omission. I had to accept his words, but I wasn't going to do it graciously.

The next day, he opened the door and nodded at me, "Good morning, Dr. Jagoe."

I followed him in and lay wordlessly on the couch for the first ten minutes. I was thinking about how I had already had my PhD for years. I remembered flying home from Durham, North Carolina back in 1998. David and Sebastian, two years old, were taking a nap together. They woke up when I walked in, and Sebastian, still groggy, reached his arms up and said, "Dr. Mama!" I cuddled him and pretended I was a medical doctor, listening to his fluttery heartbeat. "No, Mama, not that kind of doctor. A book doctor!"

David was already on the phone, calling my parents to tell them about their daughter's success. I never told them about any of my accomplishments, since it made me feel like I was showing off, begging for their approval. He would do it instead, insistent that they needed to understand that their daughter was amazing. Through his enthusiasm, they were able to get a glimmer of what I did in my life.

So why hadn't I corrected Dr. O for all those days that he had called me "Ms. Jagoe," a form of address that made me think only of my mother? Like him, I was a doctor. But we weren't equals. He was in a position of power over me as I lay there on the couch. I think that I had figured I could maintain some semblance of power not by asserting my title, but by hiding it from him. That way he wouldn't know what I really was. I could be his patient, and invest him with the authority of doctor.

He waited silently for me to say something. I shrugged again, determined to not think about how I had abdicated my accomplishments. I had allowed his form of address to interpellate me into a lesser and gendered position. I had given away the title that I had worked for years to achieve. I thought how David would correct him immediately. God, it would be awful to have David in that room, talking fast and furious about me, especially if it was in the admiring tone that he often used. I knew then that I wasn't going to let any part of him monopolize this analysis. I was going to have to disclose the different facets of myself to Dr. O on my own. And keep, for as long as I could, my marriage out of the discussion.

When Dr. O called me "Dr. Jagoe," our relationship shifted. I had always known that we were two doctors sitting in that room. Now he knew it too.

Take Her

Dolores was visiting me and David and the boys. She was quite old by then, and had trouble with her bunions and her arthritic back. She had been coming to stay with us for long periods of time ever since Sebastian was a newborn in our tiny apartment in Princeton, where she slept on the couch for three months. She was good at erasing the traces of her presence, so that when we woke up, she'd already cleaned the bathroom after using it, and put away her blanket and pillow.

The first days of any of her visits were always the most difficult. She immediately took over the kitchen, rearranging the cabinets so that she could reach the items she used the most. Liam would do flying leaps off the furniture, or he and Sebastian would wrestle and shriek, and Dolores would gasp and cry *"Ay no, papito!"* as David and I would try to reassure her that they were just playing. We'd only settle into a more equanimous routine once I gave into her way of doing things. I'd stop telling her that the kids didn't need her to make *pupusas* every day, that their t-shirts didn't need ironing, and that I didn't like them drinking so much juice. They adored her, and I knew we were lucky to have her there. Even if it meant that in the evenings, instead of hanging out with David after the kids were asleep, I would be sitting with her, watching a *telenovela* or listening to stories from her childhood. I was the only person she could really talk to in our house, so when I came home from work she was desperate for me.

Her visit made me start talking about her in analysis. I told Dr. O the story I had heard so often, about when I was born and brought home from hospital. My siblings crowded around my parents to see the new baby, but my father handed me to Dolores, the housekeeper that had recently arrived from El Salvador. He said, "Take her, she's yours."

My parents always insisted that he said it as a joke. But they hadn't wanted more children. They were strict Catholics so they didn't use birth control. All six pregnancies were unplanned. The two miscarriages between my siblings were a relief to my mother. She didn't want children in the first place, and suffered from postpartum depression after all our births.

Dr. O said, "She didn't want children…."

When he echoed my words like this, it had the effect of making me hear the words I had just uttered.

I said, "A child should never know that she was unwanted."

I really felt it at that moment: that the whole time I was growing in her womb she saw me as an intrusion. Had I always known that?

"Dolores certainly wanted me though," I said. "Do you know that "Dolores" means "pains" in Spanish? Oh my god, she was definitely in pain. Her own children had been raised by an older sister because Dolores was an unwed teen. Dolores lived as the poor relation in her siblings' homes, caring for and doting on their children, while her own grew up far from her. When she came to my family at age 50, she was finally making a new life for herself, sponsored by my parents to be a legal worker in the United States. So I guess she had to prove herself indispensable. She kept the house immaculate, made all the meals, did the laundry, and took care of the kids."

"Like she's doing for you now?" Dr. O said.

"No, it's so different! With us, she's family. The boys see how affectionate I am with her, and they adore her. She does whatever she wants, I don't treat her like a servant!"

I had a certain phrase of hers running through my head, but didn't say it to Dr. O. It was what she said to David at the dinner table, when he tried to offer her more food in his rudimentary Spanish. She would push the serving bowl back to him, saying that it was all for him: *"Suyo, suyo, suyo!"* which is the formal form of saying "Yours, yours, yours." David and I teased each other with this phrase, the epitome of her self-abnegation in the service of others, as we would try to push the last bite of a treat on each other.

Dolores lived in my parents' house for twenty-five lonely years. She was separated from her family and country and language. She was often treated, by my mother, by my siblings, and sometimes by me, as a necessary nuisance. My mother resented Dolores's presence, even though she relied on her. My siblings were ill at ease with her and jealous of the attention that she gave me. They hated when she swooped in to whisk me away from their rough play. Because my father insisted that they behave with her, they took out their anger on me, teasing me for my

Salvadorean Spanish. They told me stories about the good old days before my birth disrupted the order of things. "Spoiled" was the epithet most often hurled at me, as if I were food that had been rendered inedible because of some excess of flavor or temperature or time.

I probably did act spoiled, screaming in rage at them with a Spanglish string of words that caused them to taunt me more. Dolores would come running to protect me from their fists and words, and I hid in her arms, safe until the next time they caught me alone. Her hovering presence reinforced my belief that I couldn't live without her protection, or without her songs, stories, food, and constant physical affection. Simultaneously smothered and loved, I couldn't differentiate between being spoiled and being nourished.

This account of Dolores, like the ocean story, is such a distillation! I didn't tell it the way I'm writing it now. I shuddered and heaved and cried and writhed over a period of weeks before I could even hear it. I can't write it that way, because I don't remember the hesitancies and equivocations that it took to get there. I did take notes after many sessions, but they always rendered the half-said things into something coherent. They didn't capture what it was like to hit up against the pain and fear and incomprehension that I regularly encountered on the couch.

I do know that we kids intuited that there was something wrong with our family. No one else in the Washington suburbs had a live-in housekeeper. We had a non-family member in our house who folded everyone's underwear and wiped noses and held the heavy dish steady in her shaking hands as we served ourselves at the dining-room table. She ate in the kitchen. The pastel short-sleeved uniforms with aprons that she wore daily were bought in Spain by my mother every summer. Dolores called my parents "Señor" and "Doña Eva," which sounded like "Doñeva" when she meekly asked her if she could clear the dishes. She called me "Mami," a Central American term of endearment. The kids in the neighborhood teased me about being the mommy of a grown woman.

No wonder I so often read the Rapunzel fairy tale in which a child is given by her parents to a covetous older spinster. I was especially intrigued by the beginning, in which a married couple longs for years to have children. When the wife finally becomes pregnant, she develops a longing for a leafy rapunzel that grows in her neighbor's garden. Her husband sneaks over and gathers some of the greens, which revive her until the craving returns. She falls ill. The husband sneaks over the wall again. This time he is discovered by the witch who lives in the house. When he pleads that his wife will die without the plant, the witch tells him to take as much as he wants, as long as he gives her the baby that his wife is carrying. He agrees.

Parents are always such screw-ups in fairytales. They lose their children. They give them away. They forsake them. Maybe the parents aren't just being careless. Maybe they don't, in fact, want their children. In old wives' lore, rapunzel is thought to induce abortion. That gives a more sinister twist to the Rapunzel story. It could be that the mother wants to terminate her pregnancy. Or that she is so sick that she and her husband are willing to give the child up. Having a kid isn't everything parents imagine it will be. Rapunzel's future parents may want to be free of that burden at whatever cost.

So they abandon their child. She is given to the witch — "Take her, she's yours." The witch wants her so much that she confines her to a tower so that no one else can see her beauty. Rapunzel's golden tresses are used by the lonely woman as a ladder. Rapunzel seems to have been gracious about lowering down her hair. It must have hurt, though, to have someone pull her hair like that.

Over the days that I talked about Rapunzel to Dr. O, a memory came to me. Dolores was dressing me for church one Sunday when I was about seven. She had buttoned my dress up the back and pulled up my white stockings. All that was left was to put my hair in pigtails. She loved my light brown hair. She said it was like silk with *hilos de oro,* threads of gold. I hated having it brushed though. I'd squirm and complain while she tried to untangle it. The brush snagged on yet another knot, and I grabbed the brush out of her hand. I threw it across the room, screaming at her. As she knelt to get it from under the table, I was flooded with shame at my tantrum. I thought she would start trembling or crying, the way she did when my mother got angry with her. Instead, she hugged me, and said, "I know it hurts, Mamita. I'm trying not to pull."

"Rapunzel, Rapunzel, let down your hair?" mused Dr. O.

I nodded. It's like I was Dolores's ladder. I was the only way she could get a foothold in the house. Every morning, she was on tenterhooks when she took my mother her breakfast in bed. I gauged my mother's temper that day by checking whether Dolores's cheeks were flushed. Sometimes her voice shook as she said, "When I asked your mother what to make for dinner, she snapped at me." I'd be scared then too. I wouldn't want to go say goodbye to her before the carpool picked me up. Dolores would push me to go up.

I'd peer around her bedroom door and see my mother, propped up in bed with the tray on her lap, flipping wearily through the *Washington Post*. Her discontent was as palpable as the satin on her dressing gown, the crumbs on the sheets as I leaned over to kiss her soft cheek. She said, "Dolores drives me crazy. She wants me to plan dinner before I've even had my first sip of orange juice." I looked down at the Wedgewood teacup and saucer, the toast in the toast rack, the butter and marmalade, and the fluted juice glass. All untouched. It looked like this was going to be one of her unhappy days. I took a sip of the fresh-squeezed juice though I had just brushed my teeth, and said, "Mmmm, you should try it."

"Double life?" said Dr. O. There it was again, the phrase he had said the first day I met him.

I thought of the poet Bhanu Kapil's question: "Who was responsible for the suffering of your mother?"[3] I was always aware of each of those woman's suffering, and how much each caused the other's. They were two Hispanic women, foreigners in the suburbs that circumscribed their existence. They seemed trapped in a cycle of resentment and mutual suspicion, like they couldn't possibly trust each other. Dolores needed me to be her sole confidante in that household.

As I got older, however, I began to see how their suffering was caused by something much larger than each other. And that their relationship, though fraught, was also surprisingly intimate. It was to my mother that Dolores confided details about her children's father, the young son of her wealthy relative, who was expected to marry a woman of his class though he was allowed to get her pregnant twice. To me, she often told stories about El Salvador, but never mentioned her sexual experiences, even when I was a teen myself. I was her beautiful girl, her responsibility, her hope, her love, her champion, but I was not privy to the pain that shaped and defined her. That was something that my mother, entrapped in her own isolation, could understand, could share. Me, I made her feel necessary and indispensable. I was hers.

Shortcut

After only the first month of my analysis, the Latin American Studies Association met in Rio de Janeiro. I dithered about whether to withdraw from the panel on Argentine contemporary cinema. It seemed so disruptive to leave the analysis so soon after starting it. On the other hand, I didn't want to hurt my career or my visibility. I decided to go for only two nights.

I slept badly in the cheap hotel, kept up in part by the snoring of the portly specialist in Ecuadorian silent film with whom I was sharing the room. The first night, I had a dream about a boy in a detention center. He tried to escape by crossing a line. Immediately a big guard pushed him to the ground. The boy fought back but the guard put his knee hard on his chest, ramming his elbow in the boy's ear. Overpowered, the boy went limp. The guard dragged him over the line, exiling him to the desert. The fight was broken out of him. The boy's sobs reverberated through the desert, long loud notes of despair, deep and old and inconsolable. There would be no end to his crying.

I woke in the middle of the night with the sound of his sobs still echoing through me. They seemed both cathartic and unbearable, a necessary release that was too awful to witness. The dream felt like it was about my analysis. Dr O. was my jailer, pressing on my ear to make me hear my own words. If I stopped resisting, I too would be broken. A timeless and unassuageable sadness within me would be unleashed. It was always there, lurking just below my frenetic fight to cross lines and run away.

The next morning, I went to a panel on psychoanalysis in Latin America, and made a comment about the transferential relationship between analyst and analysand. I sounded smart. I knew I had made an impression on one academic in particular. He and I had always liked talking to each other at conferences. We went out for a drink. It was my last night before I went back to David and the boys and the dog and cat in our rambly, messy, dirty house. Before I returned to the classroom and to committee meetings and publication deadlines. Before I once again lay on Dr. O's couch and had to endure his implacable listening. We flirted. We had another drink. I suggested a walk on the beach. There, in the moonlight, we kissed, pressing up against each other with the hunger of two people who had been well-behaved spouses and parents and professors for a long time. He was burly and solid, unlike my lanky David, and I was completely turned on by the thick bulge pressing against my leg. I went back to my hotel room excited and frustrated.

That night, I once again had a vivid dream. David told me to take a shortcut through the desert and a snake came after me, a big one. I couldn't believe that a snake would chase a human. I had to do something, so I grabbed it by the head as it tried to bite me with its big teeth. I yelled to a kid nearby to go get my husband. As I waited for him to come, I got a handle on the snake, pacifying it with my strong grip. I went back to the camp with the snake in my fist. David was surrounded by children who were listening to his funny stories. He looked up with surprise, just then remembering that he was supposed to come rescue me.

I wanted my husband to defend me from the bite of a *snake*? Come on, how obvious could my unconscious get, that I hoped that my marital state would contain me enough to not act on the temptation? That morning, before I got on the plane, the man and I met in his hotel room and hurriedly undressed before his roommate got back from breakfast. Dreamily, I grabbed his cock by the head because it had pursued me with its bulging importuning. I had to get it under control so that it would chase me no more.

As if. Our desire for each other was visceral and intense and it caught me unawares. We pleasured each other without penetration, and it felt more alive than I had felt in ages. Afterwards, as we strolled on the Copacabana promenade, we imagined an alternate life in which we lived together there, talking, fucking, turning each other on with our minds and bodies. But on the plane back I knew, despite my erotic reveries, that there was only one life, and in that one I was trying not to be the kind of person who acted on such impulses anymore.

Much later, Dr. O told me that I presented myself, in the first consultation meetings, as someone who has affairs. I denied it categorically, telling him that I couldn't have said that, because of the relationship that David and I had. For the first decade, we had been open. Certain that we were going to be together for life, we decided not to limit our sexual experiences to just the other. Two years before I started analysis, David and I had separated, getting back together six months later. In that second round of the marriage, we decided to swear off other people. When I first started going to analysis, I was monogamous and trying desperately to believe in my marriage. Therefore, I told Dr. O, there was no way that I would have classified any extramarital encounters I had in that first decade as "affairs." Brazil was my first one.

After some months, though, I began to suspect that Dr. O was right. Maybe I had in fact said that I was someone who had affairs. Even though my marriage had been polyamorous for so long, the few men I slept with were in monogamous relationships. The dynamic was always one of seduction, transgression, and resistance overcome. Part of the breathless exhilaration of the first touch was the feeling that I was irresistible, that they were willing to forego their morals, their promises, and their loyalty to the wife just to have sex with me. The romantic fantasy was always as exciting as the physical discoveries.

When I came back from Brazil and lay on the couch, I felt dirtier, more aroused, and giddier than anything I had yet displayed in my analysis. I recounted minute details of the smell and taste of the seduction. He said nothing. Then I told him about the snake dream.

He said, "Shortcut?"

I had no idea what he was talking about. I had cheated on my husband, and he chose to concentrate on one word from a dream? But I was starting to trust his questions. If I allowed myself to respond, we usually got at the undercurrents of whatever story I thought I was telling. The unconscious fears and motivations that shaped my actions emerged through these circumlocutory conversations.

So I said the first thing that came to my mind: "David and I have been taking a shortcut ever since we got back together. We want the marriage to work. All the problems that made us split up before are still there. So we're avoiding them, trying so hard to be a good husband and wife. But maybe I can't be a good wife. Maybe this is who I am. Someone who can't be monogamous, who has an 'obscene desire.'"

This wording was actually from a line in the philosopher Alain Badiou's *Ethics,* in which he says that there is always the temptation to leave a loving relationship because of the "pull of an obscene desire."[4] I had been thinking about that phrase, wondering how you know whether the new thing is an event that demands your ethical response and openness to it, or if it is an escapist fantasy that pulls you away from what you should persevere in.

I was about to get on a roll about how I seemed to be incapable of being good, when Dr. O cut me off, saying, "You like to spiral into being self-critical."

"Why do you think I'm being critical? Maybe it's objectively true. Maybe I am someone who is incapable of loyalty. Look at my track record. The last couple of years of monogamy are the anomaly, not the norm."

At that moment, I didn't get what he was saying. It was easier to shrug my shoulders and say, "I'm the kind of person that…," than to think more about why I did the things I did. It was an easy shortcut.

Later in the session, he said, "Maybe this sexual encounter is an enactment for analysis, a kind of staging to see what happens, how I react, if I kick you out."

I shuddered, because this had been my sneaking fear; that being in analysis had made me do something illicit, that it had made me worse instead of better.

"Or," he continued, "there's another interpretation, which is that you went to another continent to take offshore something that you needed to express, an obscene desire that you don't want us to ignore but that you have to keep separate."

I started to cry. "I don't want there to be two versions of what I did. I want it to be one or the other. Just tell me if I am a good wife or a slut. Am I a promiscuous coward who is running away from analysis, or am I trying to express parts of myself that I fear?"

This kind of either/or thinking was, I learned over time, the most well-trodden shortcut of my psyche. It was like the Rubin vase optical illusion, impossible for me to hold two perspectives at once. I would see the vase or I would see two faces mirrored. White was the ground and black the figure, or vice versa, but I could not see both at once.

The longer path was beginning to emerge. One in which I would have to accept that the image contains both face and vase, that within me were contradictory desires and behaviors. In the slow and hard work of analysis, I caught glimpses of that path — arduous, slow, unavoidable — stretching out before me. Already in the first month, analysis had changed something, made it possible or thinkable for me to bring the "obscene desire" into the same space as the "good."

At the end of the month, he handed me an envelope. As soon as I left his office, I opened it and unfolded the thick creamy paper, embossed with his name and address across the top. There, in old-fashioned cursive written with a fountain pen, was his bill of $507.63 for the three missed days.

Virgin Mary

My mother once said that it must have been the care and love that I received from Dolores that made me the most carefree of the four of us children. For many years, I believed what she said, that having had a surrogate mother had freed me of the weight of my mother's postpartum depression and enabled me to flourish. I figured that Dolores had been my "good-enough mother." That term comes from the psychoanalyst D.W. Winnicott.[5] His theory is that children will grow up stable and independent, able to withstand the losses and separations of social life, if they are cared for by someone who is there for them, who is strong enough to be able to withstand their rage and anger without being undone by it. Dolores proved that to me when I threw the hairbrush.

Yet Dolores was not "good enough" for me because she only fulfilled the first part of Winnicott's theory: the total responsiveness that she gave me as a baby. The next step should have been to move gradually away so that I could learn to tolerate her inattention and her absence. Instead, she stayed very close, rarely leaving me alone. Maybe she was trying to fill my yearning for attention from my biological mother. The fact that my mother sometimes cuddled me when I sat next to her on the couch, or dressed me in an outfit that matched hers, only raised my hopes and confused matters. Which of the two women was going to give me enough care *and* enough inattention to be good enough?

My mother was raised in a patriarchal bourgeois pro-Franco household in the rigid years after the Spanish Civil War. She had never lived without domestic live-in service. My father had also grown up being cared for by black domestic workers in Mississippi. With four children, they considered it essential to have a live-in housekeeper even though my mother didn't work. We children believed the logic: my mother was too fragile and too elegant to clean the house; we were too much for her to handle; and our needs could only be met by someone who was hired to do so. What made it so confusing was that, despite my mother's distance and formal use of *Usted* when she talked to her, Dolores was so integral to our family and to our home.

This dynamic was most pronounced in a country in which both women's language was spoken. We all went to Spain every summer, to my mother's family country estate outside Barcelona. All winter, in the suburbs of Washington, I counted the days until we went back, imagining every moment of our arrival — Puig the chauffeur's pomaded hair and wreath of cigar smoke as we drove past the post-war social housing towers that lined the *autopista,* the long dirt road through the woods that led up to the tall wrought iron gates, the ponderous squeak as the *masovero* opened them and the dogs swarmed the car barking, the first glimpse of the flaking stucco of the tall mansion, the hugs of my many blonde cousins in their matching bathing suits, their warm skin exuding the scent of chlorine and cologne.

At that old Catalan *finca,* the social order was clearly established, and implicitly accepted by everyone involved. The maids, gardeners, cooks, and nannies had their free time at siesta time. They gathered in the courtyard to smoke and tell raunchy stories, complaining about being stuck out in the country. We kids clustered around them, learning about sex and intrigues and families so different from ours. As a young teen, I eagerly copied their slang and took puffs of their tarry dark Ducados cigarettes, teasing them about their beaus and doing chicken dances around them.

Dolores never took part in those sessions. She went to her room and rested her feet, swollen from the summer heat. She tried to keep me with her, because she thought the Spanish maids were ordinary and crass. She didn't want me to talk like them, especially since they swore *coño* all the time, a word that means "cunt" but is used in Spain the way "fuck" is here. I loved the word, and the emphasis with which it was said. For their part, the Spanish servants thought she was unfriendly and a snob. She was rigid in her hierarchies, disparaging cooks who were uppity, maids who didn't know how to polish silverware properly, and seamstresses who flirted with gardeners.

Dolores hated the *finca*. Back in the United States, she had an exceptional status in our household. In Spain the hired help were treated as employees, not family or friends. Gloria, the maid who had been working for my aunt for over twenty years, would hover silently over the dining table, holding a tray of food with white gloves, her presence barely acknowledged as the adults gossiped about the Vendrell family. Mercedes and Pilar would feed the children an early dinner, bathe them, and dress them in their matching pajamas so they could go out to the garden to kiss their parents goodnight before being tucked in by the nannies. As soon as the kids were in bed, the two women could go smoke on the back patio with the cooks and the drivers, while their employers smoked and drank wine on the front patio.

More even than back in Washington, I felt embarrassed by Dolores's solicitude and over-protectiveness. The other nannies followed the children to wipe their faces, scold them for dirtying their clothes, or march them off to the playroom for their lunch. They didn't share their secrets or break down in tears in front of them. They didn't try to get the kids on their side against the adults. So I avoided Dolores as much as I could, hiding in the garden or in the attic and cringing when I heard her *Mami*?

At night, though, we slept in the same room. She lay in the little bed while I fidgeted in the big canopy bed in the cavernous room. In the dark, I could sense the big painting that hung on the wall across from me. A religious painting of the Virgin Mary, her heart exposed. As a Catholic girl at a Sacred Heart school, I was familiar with the long-suffering patient face of the Virgin, the halo framing her head. In the *finca* painting, she looked directly at me as she drew her blue cape open and pointed with one finger to a red visceral heart, light beams radiating out from it.

"Look," the Virgin seemed to gesture. "Here's my throbbing vulnerable heart! Take it if you want."

She was so provocative as she parted her clothes and exposed her little red secret. By showing that which shouldn't be seen, she was giving it all — her pain and her passion. I'd roll the beads of the rosary between my fingers and pray the "Hail Mary" while I waited for Dolores to begin to snore. Then I'd turn over onto my stomach and find my own little red organ exposed between the folds. Touching it soothed me, smoothing the edges of the dichotomies that hummed below the surface of my days playing in the pool with my cousins. Family versus servants, mother versus nanny, Europe versus America. My tall boyish body versus my adorable girl cousins in their smocked dresses. My *sudaca* accent versus the Castilian lisp of their *c*'s and *z*'s.

I didn't know what it was that I was doing when I touched myself in the dark. It was a secret ritual that only I had. Until the day that I woke early to notice movement in the little bed next to me. Dolores was doing the same thing that I did, I could tell by the rhythms. I was both repulsed and reassured. Since I only knew it as a mechanism for coping with the incongruities of my situation, I recognized, on some level, how hard it was for her as well. Neither of us fit into either our home in Washington or the beautiful *finca*. But she was a grown up, and I needed her to have figured it out, to not have such a hot desperate urge. Named after the Virgin of the Pains, Dolores, in that moment, exposed her vulnerable and pained heart to me. I didn't want to know. She was supposed to be the adult who took care of me. Instead, she was filled with an inchoate and possessive anxiety that far exceeded the parameters of the waged labor she performed. She wasn't able to gently and consistently let go of me the way that a good-enough mother would. She took what was given to her and held on tight.

Where the Couch Was

Dr. O's office was in a predominantly white and affluent area of Toronto with the kinds of mediocre butcher shops, cafes, and gourmet food delis that middle-aged conservatives like. No hipster craft beer, locally roasted coffee, or artisanal shops had infiltrated those established commercial stretches. His house was on a broad residential street of old trees and single-family homes. Lexuses and Mercedes parked in the driveways. Over the five years of trudging down it, I associated Dury Avenue with:

durability;

duration;

the *longue durée*;

Drury Lane, as in where the Muffin Man lives;

and, most strongly, through some careless amalgamation of nursery rhymes:

"Run, run, as fast as you can! You can't catch me, I'm the Gingerbread Man!"

I would walk down the driveway to the side of Dr. O's house, taking in details of his domestic space without allowing myself to know that I was — the carefully tended plants, the transparent daisy curtains, the seasonal wreath and holiday decorations. All maintained, I imagined, by a wife, someone who tastefully cared for the household by spending the money garnered by her husband's protracted labor in the basement.

He must have saved a lot of money by not having a consultancy outside of the house. Once I opened the outer door as he was standing in the threshold from the main floor. Behind him I saw gleaming kitchen appliances and a solid granite-topped kitchen island. His head was turned back to address an older Latina woman who was hunched over the vacuum cleaner. In his hand was a tupperware with a thermos balanced on top of it. I didn't see what was in it, so I never knew if he ate sandwiches or salad or leftovers in the short intervals between patients. From that glimpse I had learned that he ate his lunch in the basement instead of in the kitchen or dining room. I wondered if that was his own decision, or a rule imposed by his wife, who wanted him out of the house.

Dr. O demarcated the boundaries between work and home so strictly. Even though we could hear the sound of footsteps or the vacuum cleaner above our heads, he never spoke of his household. He kept his own family concerns, his sexual relationship, his domestic circumstances, out of the space of our session.

Like Dolores had. All the compartments, the things that could not be spoken. When we were alone in her basement room, she sometimes complained about my mother, but other times told me how wonderful and generous she was. I hushed her when *Happy Days* came on. Letting me watch TV was one of her small acts of rebellion against my parents, whose rule was an hour of television a week. Sometimes my father came down when he got home from work and caught me, my mouth full of the After Eight mints she bought me on her days off. He would tell me not to be a nuisance to Dolores, and I would skulk up the stairs to do my homework.

When I had bad dreams in the middle of the night, I crept down to her room. I feared my parents catching me more than I feared the absolute darkness of the basement, so I never turned on a light. I groped my way down the stairs, gripping the banister tightly, until I opened the door to her chilly room. Enough light came in from the bedroom window to see her face and sparse hair wrapped around plastic curlers. I'd lean over and kiss her cheek, cold to my lips. For a brief instant, I imagined she was dead. I was alone with a corpse. Then she'd murmur my name and open the bed sheets so I could snuggle up to her warm body.

About these middle-of-the-night trips, Dr. O said, "Upstairs, downstairs...."

On other nights, she'd sneak up to my room, against my parents' request that she stay downstairs after dinner so that I spoke English with my siblings. She told me stories and sang to me till I fell asleep. We'd hear my father in my sister's bedroom, and know that it meant that he had decided to check on each of us that night. She would slip into the dark bathroom as he opened the door, listening while he sang to me and stroked my back.

I'm pretty sure he knew she was in there, but her never called her out. I feigned sleep so that he'd leave more quickly. He was an intruder into our secret alliance. The feeling of her discomfort from the shadows was more pressing than the touch of his hand on my skin.

As Dolores hovered over even the quiet moments that I spent alone with my father, she acted as a constant reminder that I shouldn't trust my family, who hadn't wanted me. Every time my siblings complained about her, or my mother was angry with her, she must have, like Rapunzel's captor, reinforced our isolation and bond by tugging on the golden link between us.

I lay on Dr. O's couch and closed my eyes, remembering the velvety dark of the stairs to Dolores's basement room. I felt the terror of groping my way in that pitch black subterranean space, and, simultaneously, the comfort of succumbing to the complete darkness. To not rely on my sight was to instead take note of the invisible atmosphere that surrounded me, to feel the ground beneath me and the air around me.

The space of Dr O's office also required a different form of attention. I was learning to notice not just what lay obviously on the surface. I was tentatively feeling my way into a darkness within me. That was where I went when I descended the steps into the basement of the house on Dury.

Selkie

Propped against the back wall of my father's wardrobe was a photo of my mother, standing on the Costa Brava coast. Squinting in the bright sun, lips open, her smile is self-conscious but not strained as it is in most photos. She is radiant as the sun gleams on her oiled shoulders and legs, the bathing suit taut as it fifties-contours her body. Sometimes my father took down the framed photo and we stared at it, marveling at her youth and how happy she looked. She would pooh-pooh us, saying "Ay, look how fat I was!" That layer of voluptuous curve was, it is true, gone from the woman who had moved to America and become my thin and unhappy mother.

In that photo, she is in her element. Like the selkie of Celtic folklore, she is most gleaming and alive by the sea, but taken far away from it she seemed to fade. The selkie is a seal who once a year swims to the shore at nighttime and wriggles out of her thick dark sealskin. The revealed body is that of a human woman, naked, beautiful. If a man manages to take her sealskin, she will follow him. And if he can hide it from her, he will possess her and she will remain with him, wife and mother to their human children. Her eyes, though, always reveal the captive animal within, so that even when she looks at her human family she is divided, never quite present to them. It is common knowledge that if she finds that skin, the selkie will put it on and go directly back into the sea, where she will become a seal again and not risk coming on land.

In some versions, it is the daughter of this inter-species couple that finds the pulsating animal skin stuffed in the back of her father's closet. I imagine the girl instantly attracted to it, smelling and touching it and draping it around her shoulders. Like when I buried myself in my mother's closet and caress her furs, breathing in their animal smell mixed with the scent of Nina Ricci's L'Air du Temps. My mother's coats were gifts given to her by her parents and my father, expensive heavy garments that she wore often in her attempts to fend of the American cold. They made her look richly cared for and well-bred. When I tried them on over my t-shirt and shorts, they molded themselves around my bare skin, their weight an embrace.

The mythic daughter, little knowing the repercussions of her action, takes the heavy skin into the kitchen. Her mother's drooping head perks up as she sees it. She grabs it and drapes it around her, burrowing into its folds to arise up transformed, gleaming, coursing with life. Without even a sidelong glance, a nod of gratitude, a farewell, she turns her back on her daughter and returns to the sea.

Ooze

I started psychoanalysis in spring, which meant that I hadn't been going for that long before Dr. O took his long summer holiday. I knew it was coming, but as the time drew near, I began to panic. I felt that he was punishing me for my bad behavior at the conference. I also feared what I would do while he was gone. What if I couldn't care for myself properly? What if I couldn't cope with his absence and went wild or crazy?

I told him that my sister said that every time one of us was born, our parents went on a holiday when we were six weeks old. It wasn't till I had my own children that I understood why. Six weeks is when they tell you that you can have sex again. So my parents must have gone off to the Virgin Islands or Hawaii to reaffirm their relationship as lovers and adults, without the burden of the baby or the chore of breastfeeding.

"Can you imagine?" I said to Dr. O. "There's no way I would have been able to leave my own six-week old babies. If I was away from them for more than a couple of hours, my breasts ached and I felt like I was missing a part of my body. How could my parents have flown away for a week and left a newborn? What would a newborn feel at such a desertion?"

"What indeed? What did *you* feel?"

I began to cry in the heavy silence that followed his question.

He said, "We are enacting a similar disruption early in the analysis." (I wish I could make audible the matter-of-fact, quiet, unassuming way he said it. He did use those exact words — that was how he talked. Like he was gently, thoughtfully, reading from a book.) "I'm leaving soon after we've started. You are still, so to speak, in the newborn phase of our time together."

I heard this as sympathy, which part of me wanted and needed from him, but another part rejected. The next day I began the session by saying, "I don't want you to worry about me. I don't want you to like me. All I want from you is constancy. But I don't know how to secure your constancy without making you worry about me. Or fall in love with me."

He said, "It seems that you learned a life lesson that you have to keep others on track. You can't just go about your business because they may slip away from you."

That week, I was tired, felt like I was underwater. My gut churned with anxiety as I lay on the couch, embarrassing me with its loud gurgling. I hoped to hush it by not drinking coffee before the session. When that didn't work, I tried first making sure my stomach was full, then that it was empty. I'd talk over it to drown it out, but we both heard it in that quiet room where we listened to everything. When he commented on it, I remembered how he had said, at the second consultation, that he thought I would be a good candidate for analysis because I was "talkative." My mother had complained of this, that I exhausted and irritated her with my talking. I felt immense shame and disgust at myself. Shit, why couldn't I shut up? Even my gut had to talk. I had hoped to do something different in analysis, to be more controlled and less needy, but instead I was becoming ever more abject. I was incapable of hiding my shameful attributes.

Lying there worrying about my digestive sounds, I all of a sudden began to laugh, really belly laugh, as I remembered a scene from Charlie Chaplin's *Modern Times*. The Tramp sits in a quiet room next to an affluent and proper woman. He is ill at ease in such a prim setting, and attempts to smile and ingratiate himself to her, but she stares coldly down her nose at him, so he shrugs his shoulders and sips his tea. She does the same, and the camera focuses on her as a loud and long gurgling sound begins. She looks startled and uncomfortable. Her little dog barks at her stomach. And then the Tramp's stomach also gurgles.

I had just taught a graduate seminar on early cinema, and knew that the Lumière Brothers first film screened in 1895, the same year as the publication of Freud and Bauer's *Studies on Hysteria*. Film critics have made much of this coincidence, because film and psychoanalysis share a common attribute: they both make it possible to see things that had not been seen before. Writing about these early films, the philosopher and critic Walter Benjamin says that they mark the beginning of a new age because "the camera introduces us to unconscious optics as does psychoanalysis to unconscious impulses."[6] What he means is that the camera allows us to see things that had heretofore passed by our eyes since we were unable to slow down or zoom in enough to know what was happening right in front of us. And psychoanalysis, too, brings into focus what which has not been noticed before. Like the sound of a gut.

In 1936, when both *Modern Times* and Benjamin's essay came out, the actor and the writer both had deep knowledge of what had been rendered possible by film and its images. But at that moment, sound was beginning to be used in film. With the gurgling guts, I think that Chaplin introduces us to unconscious *acoustics*. The Tramp, that recognizable silent figure whose body did all the expressing, still does not speak, but that does not mean that he is silent: his stomach tells a story of its own. Try as he might to act in the proper way, there is another truth that is demanding to assert itself: a truth about the power dynamics that repeatedly reinforce his outsider status. His character may resist speaking, but Chaplin the director forces him into sound anyway, embarrassing him by making his discomfort audible.

The Tramp tries to cover up the sound of his stomach by turning on the nearby radio, which tunes into an announcer asking, "Do you suffer from gastritis?" He quickly turns it off again. He and his audience are being forced to become conscious of these acoustics that have always already been there. They were just more easily ignored before they were amplified by new sound technologies.

I felt like the Tramp. I'd been going through my life thinking that I was hiding my discomfort, even though, like him, it was probably displayed in every gesture, grimace, and movement of my body. I thought I was good at seeming cool when I was flustered, or in control when I was actually feeling threatened and vulnerable. Perhaps others saw right through me, but I didn't. Until now. Until my insides were being exposed by this new method, this technology of psychoanalysis which was making the unconscious conscious. We were listening to it manifest itself through my stutters, my word choices, and even my insides. It was exactly what Freud described: "He that has eyes to see and ears to hear may convince himself that no mortal can keep a secret. If his lips are silent, he chatters with his fingertips; betrayal oozes out of him at every pore."[7]

I did, while Dr. O was gone, go about my business and keep my husband, children, and colleagues on track. I basically felt like I'd forgotten about analysis until the morning of his return, when I woke up with stomach cramps. (The sudden cramp of bowels, brought on by the anxiety of going to a session, led me to mentally map, over the years, every public restroom between the subway and his office).

When I arrived, I was angry. I said, "Analysis is something you do when you are discontented. I, thank you very much, feel content. I'm fine in my marriage. I'm a good mother. Analysis could be dangerous to all that."

"Analysis," he responded, not rising to the bait, "could lead you to not inhabit your house?"

I paused. I had to think about that. I became a little less hostile as I talked about what it meant to inhabit a house, inhabit a family. Before long I was crying as I realized how clenched up I'd felt the whole time, playing at being a good householder and wife and employee. "Over the hiatus, I packed with cotton the wound that analysis has opened up in me. But now we're back and you're asking me to expose the wound again. The bleeding will start afresh."

Blood, shit, and tears: yup, I was back in analysis. My secret shame and fears were oozing out of me the second that we applied the technology of perception that psychoanalysis affords.

Like a laryngoscope, it exposed parts of my insides that I kept so carefully hidden. That which I was ashamed to show; I was beginning to vomit it all out as the instrument probed my unconscious. In psychoanalytic terms, I was dealing with the anal stage. In that stage, we learn that our parents or other adults expect us to be able to control ourselves. That which is inside us is shameful and a gift. We expel it in private, or we keep it in by tightening our sphincters.[8]

So as children, we retain or excrete, and are rewarded or punished for it. We internalize that system of rewards and punishments and do it to ourselves, learning what it is okay to release and what to contain. We are praised for our ability to demarcate the lines between inside and outside, self and other. That containment actually provides us with some comfort, as we learn to expel or distance ourselves from the abject, the unsavory, the uneasy. Maybe every now and then we get some release by spilling over our container, acting out of character. But we remain very aware of that container and its boundaries, policing ourselves constantly to make sure that they still exist. Because if not, the mess will be exposed.

In psychoanalytic theory, the understanding is that if the anal stage is not completed successfully, it can result in a personality that is either too rigid or too disordered. I don't know the details of my toilet training or if they would offer me the key to understanding myself, but I was going to learn, with Dr. O, how much shit mattered. Those lessons learned in early childhood about what was acceptable, and what was not, were constitutive to my sense of self and my mode of being with others.

Native Skin

My friends' energetic American moms wore magenta and gold velour sweatsuits. My tiny tired mother wore European-tailored tweed skirts and blazers to drive the station wagon to the Safeway supermarket. She was like one of those indisposed characters in a nineteenth-century novel. When she had near-fainting episodes, I would run to get the slim bottle of Agua del Carmen for her to sip. Made by the Carmelite nuns, it smelled of rubbing alcohol and bitter herbs. Every summer she bought a new bottle to last her through the year.

In Spain, my mother was more animate and charged than I ever saw her in the United States. She had long conversations in rapid Spanish with her sisters and girlhood friends. She sighed to her mother about her faraway life. Actually though, I didn't see her that often, since we kids moved in a separate sphere from the adults. Sometimes, in the cool afternoon breeze, we hovered around their elaborate teatime, crowding them when they opened the round blue tin of Royal Dansk butter cookies. I always chose the sugar-crystalled pretzel ones. My cousin would perch her teacup and saucer on her knee as she listened to the women's conversation, but I would beg her to continue playing maiden to my prince or Wendy to my Peter Pan. Why did she want to listen to them talk about their gastrointestinal problems and medications?

Whoa, did they talk about shit! I figured it was part of the Catalan culture, considering the little figurine that we always put behind our Nativity set. *El cagonet,* or "the crapper," squats with his pants down and a little brown turd below him. At least he's not constipated like they all were, except when they got hit with the annual summer stomach bug. It seemed to be all or nothing, and it provided endless topics of detailed conversation and precise terminology. One of my boy cousins would crack them all up by telling the joke about the proper lady who goes to visit a friend. When her friend leaves the room to get the tea tray, the lady farts. The room stinks, so she points at the dog sitting under her chair and says, "your dog farted!" The hostess apologizes for him and leaves to get the sugar, and the lady lets another one rip, again blaming the dog. The third time, when she walks into the room and smells the noxious odor, the hitherto polite hostess says, "Fido, get out from under that chair, *que se te va a cagar encima!* [or she'll shit right on top of you!]" The joke tickled those constrained adults with its mix of artificial propriety, threat of released excrement, and surprise punch line of obscenity.

The tears rolled down my mother's face as she laughed and gasped for breath. She spent her winters being an American mother, using my father's terminology to ask us if we had regular "BMs" (an abbreviation, ridiculously, of "bowel movements"). But in the scatological Spanish summers, she could bandy the word *cagar* around and share stories, in her native tongue, of discomfort and impactedness. This talk of shit was a way to tell so much more that couldn't be said about the "land of liberty" in which her marriage confined her, about her entrapment in a foreign domesticity that she had never imagined as a young woman.

I watched her laugh. I liked her gestures and her turns of phrase in Spanish. I liked that when I looked at my grandmother and aunts, I saw the same shape of face and skin color that I recognized as my mother's and mine. But it also scared me, to see her in her element. I never feared that she wouldn't come back with us to the States — I guess that even as a child I could see that her family of origin was too dysfunctional for her — but I did dread the return of naked despondency in her gaze as the snows of February covered our sidewalk and driveway. I knew that upon our return I would want her Spanish skin to slip off so that she would just be with us, but that I would also yearn to see her attired in it again.

Umbrella

I came out of the subway into a torrential summer rainstorm. As I looked out from behind the door, the water was puddling and splashing down in sheets. I hated being late, but knew that if I ran for it — across the little playground, through the big parking lot behind the shops, and up Dury Avenue, I would be drenched. I pulled out my phone at 9:02, and to Dr. O's hoarse greeting, gushed that I was coming as soon as I could risk the downpour. His "I see" was dry, giving me no sympathy or reprieve.

Did he think I was making excuses? Stalling for time? Obviously he was judging me for my disorganization, since I hadn't checked the weather forecast like all the other commuters walking past me with their umbrellas raised against the deluge. There I stood, losing minutes of my session, giving him more fodder for disapproval. I waited for a break in the clouds. There was none. So I decided to stuff my cardigan in my backpack and run in my tank top and skirt. Once there I could strip off the soaking shirt and wear just the sweater.

I didn't, however, just do it. I called him first. "I'm going to brave the storm. I'll probably be soaked, so you should have a towel ready."

He just said, "I'm here."

"I just thought I should tell you in case you thought I wasn't coming for awhile and you were about to start on some other task. I'm still going to use my time with you today."

I was digging myself deeper into some demand on him that exceeded the situation, so I hung up and ran.

When I was almost there, I slowed down, not wanting to pant too much as I lay on the couch. I knew that if I felt self-conscious about my breathing I would be unable to catch my breath, which would make me more anxious. I took my soaking sandals off at the door and walked down the 5 steps. He was standing in the open door of the consulting room.

"I'll be there in a minute," I said, and ducked into the bathroom, using both hand towels to dry my calves and shoulders before I changed. He laid out, not a towel, but a scratchy wool rug, on top of the couch. My skin prickled away from it, damp and cold from the air conditioning. My toes felt numb. The rain continued outside the window as I muddled through the session, not admitting that the main thing I was thinking about was that he should offer me an umbrella to walk to the subway.

That summer, I had read the essay that would lead me to teach a full-year graduate seminar on Marcel Proust. It was Benjamin's "The Image of Proust," in which he characterized Proust as an author who relentlessly tries to get a response out of his reader. Benjamin creates a scenario to depict this Proustian demand in the form of a letter that Proust could have written:

> My dear Madam, I just noticed that I forgot my cane at your house yesterday; please be good enough to give it to the bearer of this letter. P.S. Kindly pardon me for disturbing you; I just found my cane.[9]

Not surprisingly, I misremembered the cane as an umbrella. I told Dr. O about the story, more tickled than I expected by its perfect exemplarity. The letter-writer asks and yet does not ask; demands an answer and fears that one will be given. He reaches out to the dear Madam and ramps up an increasingly anxious discourse in the face of her silence. Like my initial asking for Dr. O's phone number, the letter-writer demands not the object (which he already has, even if he doesn't know that he does) but something more excessive. He asks her to be his witness, as he performs his need for companionship and help. I read it as an audacious presumption on her time, and yet I was charmed by his attempt to create a bond with her that reminded her of his presence.

My version of the letter would have been something like:

Offer me your protection, Dr. O! I'm incapable of fending off the wetness. Stop it from soaking into me; stop it from oozing out of me; stop me from exposing myself to it.

But — don't you dare patronize me or pity me. I don't need anything from you, and I would reject it if you offered.

And — how do I know what would be okay to ask and what would be too much? After the embarrassment of asking for your phone number, I don't dare ask you for anything.

Dr. O did not offer me an umbrella. And I didn't ask for one. I just put my wet shoes on and splashed my way back to the subway.

Daddy Issues

In the dream, Dr. O says "Thursday" and from the bottom of the white porcelain tub that I'm lying in, I feel the room spin around me. I feel sick and dizzy but don't know why I'm reacting so strongly. He says it again, the spinning increases, and I blurt out, "A yellowed lampshade, red trim. Something about my father." I turn over onto my stomach and begin to vomit.

I woke up crying, surprised that I wasn't actually throwing up. Liam was sleeping between me and David, his arm flung over my neck. I reached over him and shook David awake. David was a heavy sleeper, but once awake, he was alert and sympathetic. We both disengaged ourselves from Liam's heavy limbs, and went into the back bedroom, empty since he was in the middle of painting it. As I tried to tell him the dream, my body shook, escalating into a full panic attack. He murmured soothingly as I paced around the room, shuddering and hyperventilating. When I finally calmed down, he said, "Well, the Thursday could represent the end of analysis for the week…."

That made sense to me. "Yeah, like I can't stand having to deal with my own psyche for the three days of the weekend. But the rest? All I can think of is that I had a lamp that may have looked like that, when I was really little."

He tried to elicit more out of me, but I changed the topic, beginning to nag him about how long the paint job was taking him. His face shifted from open to defensive. All of a sudden we both felt how tired we would be in the morning when the kids woke up. He went to sleep in Liam's empty bed. I went back to ours, where I lay watching Liam's eyelids fluttering as he dreamed.

In analysis for the next couple of days, I tried to free associate to see if I could uncover why the dream was so disturbing. I talked about the red floors and white walls of the old farmhouse at the *finca,* but I couldn't get at the terrifying feeling of disgust and vertigo.

About a month later, I remembered a line from Woody Allen's *Stardust Memories* and told it to Dr. O: "If I were in Poland, I'd have been a lampshade." I felt the nausea of the dream as I put it together.

"The lampshade was a strip of skin, lined with the blood left by the cut. Skinned. Flayed alive. In the dream it's connected somehow to my father. The man who has my mother's sealskin and keeps it so that she will stay with us. The strip of skin, though, is mine. The piece I would willingly cut out of my own flesh to give to him."

I talked repeatedly about my father stroking my bare back, with Dolores hovering anxiously in the shadows, watching over her precious girl. "If my life were a novel, I would uncover the memory of my father sexually molesting me during those bedtime visits. But instead all I come up with is his lack of interest and attention."

That semester, I was teaching Henry James's *The Wings of the Dove*, and I reread an essay on the novel by my PhD supervisor, Eve Kosofsky Sedgwick.[10] I was really struck by her reading of a scene in which the father rejects his daughter's offers of companionship and help. This is the scene:

> She now again felt, in the inevitability of the freedom he used with her, all the old ache, her mother's very own, that he couldn't touch you ever so lightly without setting up. No relation with him could be so short or so superficial as not to be somehow to your hurt.[11]

I never understood what this passage meant, it's so convoluted and Jamesian. Eve's reading clarifies what I wasn't seeing: that the father is queer, and doesn't respond sexually to either his daughter or his wife. The freedom he uses with her is the insouciant regard of a father who is not possessive of his daughter's sexuality, because he is not *interested* in her. As Eve says, "It is interesting that the language of sexual refusal here sounds so much like the language of sexual abuse."[12] His touch, no matter how light, always hurts.

Read this way, the novel made more sense to me than it ever had. The daughter is driven to act the way she does in the rest of the novel because of this setting up. In Eve's understanding of it, she reproduces this dynamic "in her behavior toward others — but reproduces it, ache and all, with the surplus of her own energy and interest, as sexuality." So my life *was* a novel, but a Henry James one! Because I too had been driven to respond to what felt like a rejection from my father through a reproduction of it. Without a father jealously guarding my body, I didn't get help from him in negotiating the mysterious realms of my sexuality. So I gave my body away, feeling that it mattered as little to me as it had to him.

My father's queerness, in relation to me, was not sexually oriented. It was, rather, his particular dated form of being an American, a kind of plucky, resilient Dale Carnegie mentality. When I was little, he was already in his mid-50s. He'd been a World War II bomber, and was now a public figure in Washington because of his civic engagement, philanthropic endeavors, and successful business ventures. Aggressively optimistic and industrious, he was married to a low-energy, infirm foreign wife. Despite the paid help who managed her household, she was too tired to accompany him to business dinners.

For the first decade of their marriage, he must have been excited to be married into a Spanish family, and to spend August at a beautiful old mansion in the mountains of the Costa Brava. By the time I was born, though, I think he was fed up. The family's dissolute habits, mismanaged wealth, unthinking privilege, and petty class concerns must have grated on my father's approach to life. Then along came the baby of his family, raised by a servant and unable to even speak to him in English for the first years of her life.

The chasm between us was most marked in the summers when my mother and I went to Spain early. By the time he arrived, I was totally immersed in that lifestyle. I saw him as an intruder. His resolute cheerfulness and energy made him an exotic outsider at the *finca*. He spent long hours by himself, exercising in the woods or typing in the attic. Once every few days, he emerged determined to engage with the family. He tried to enlist us in his desire to sightsee and explore the culture and history that we comfortably ignored. None of the adults wanted to go, so we children had to. We'd gather natural specimens like insects — I've always been terrified of antennae and exoskeletal legs — or mushrooms, which my mother threw away, saying they could be poisonous. From the highway, we'd see a ruined castle in the hills, and he'd lead us up the hill towards it. Tall and lean, he'd greet a tiny black-clad widow with a cheerful *Hola!* That was basically the extent of his Spanish. I remember him on one occasion towering over the uncomprehending woman and walking his fingers up his forearm, saying "*Podemos* walk around?" I was too embarrassed by him to step forward and translate. She just shrugged, threw up her hands, and walked away.

When I was seven, he got tickets to an outdoor performance on the Costa Brava by Montserrat Caballé. This time, the adults expressed interest, so he didn't have enough seats. He offered to stay behind with me. We had rarely been alone together, and I was uncomfortable. My English, still not very good, had deteriorated from being in Spain all summer. As we took a walk along the seawall, I ran ahead, shy to talk to him. He called me back to where he was standing. Hoisting me high on his shoulders, he told me to peek over the high wall into the opulent garden where Caballé was singing. I craned my neck, knowing that he wanted me to see inside. I could make out the back of Caballé's head and the audience all looking towards the singer. I ducked my head immediately, scared they would catch sight of my pigtails popping up over the wall.

I felt heavy, awkward, and ungainly on my father's shoulders, and began to slip down. As he caught me, I lied and said I'd seen her singing. I also said that I had come down because some people had pointed up at me. He seemed to want to hear that, and told the anecdote, with added embellishments, to our scandalized and amused relatives. He seemed to relish the role of mischievous New World iconoclast who both understood the prestige of a famous opera singer and was also irreverent about social niceties.

"I wonder," I said to Dr. O, "if he wanted to be inside that wall. I'm pretty certain he didn't want to be on the outside with a little half-Spanish girl on his shoulders."

Dr. O said nothing. I hated the way I was talking.

"I know I sound flat and affectless. I guess it's just that it already sounds so histrionic — 'Poor me, my father didn't want me!' I'm fine though. I don't want you to worry about my feelings."

"You seem," Dr. O said, "to be giving me images without yourself in them. For me to assemble."

The next day, I tried a different perspective. Maybe my dad *had* wanted me in those moments. I was like an instrument that allowed him to disrupt the closed Spanish ranks around him. Like one of those things that see over the wall of enemy trenches in World War II. What are they called? A periscope! They use mirrors to reflect different angles. To be able to mirror back the images that someone most wants to see: that is valuable. I learned to do that, to make my dad look and feel good. I saw how happy he was as he told the anecdote and garnered strong reactions from the family. Maybe it would make him feel good about me, about us.

Dr. O said, "You were gaining a sense of the potential value that you held as an instrument for a man's ego?"

"If I could just reflect back what he wanted, I could make him appreciate and need me. Wouldn't that be power?"

"Would it?" said Dr. O.

Self-Fashioning

Maybe because my upbringing was between two cultures and two languages, my academic interests also always grew in two parallel tracks. I did my BA at McGill in English, but I also took a Spanish Latin American Women's Literature class. I was captivated by Isabel Allende's stories, and tried hard to express my new feminist ideas in my household Spanish. Years later, when I was a Spanish prof myself, I learned that students like me are called heritage speakers. Their comprehension usually exceeds their capacity to talk since they lack basic grammar and vocabulary, but they effortlessly use complicated tenses such as the subjunctive.

I couldn't really express myself intellectually in Spanish, and I couldn't write it beyond the level of the chatty letters I wrote to my favorite cousin. So I never thought of majoring in Spanish. Besides, I loved English. I was especially excited by the class in Literary Theory that was a requirement for Honors English. What I learned about Marxism and deconstruction led me to do a Masters in critical and cultural theory in Wales, and then a PhD at Duke University, which, in the early 1990s, was seen as a hotbed of theory.

In my first year of the English PhD, I took Eve Sedgwick's Victorian Literature course. She obviously loved the novels that I had obsessively reread as a girl. And the ways that she analyzed the period and the writing made me feel like I had really found my calling. Up until then, my love for George Eliot and the Brontës had seemed like a secret indulgence, something that the theory boys would have rolled their eyes at. But here was the most intellectually acute and insightful woman I had ever met, lingering over the nuances of *Jane Eyre,* a book I read eleven times when I was young.

I still found myself attracted to courses in the Spanish department, though, and was much more excited by debates about post-dictatorial mourning, memory, and politics than I was in theories of the novel or poststructuralism. One evening, after David and I had gone to the climbing gym and gorged ourselves on burritos, we browsed a used bookstore in Chapel Hill. I came across Frances Bond Head's 1824 travel account, *Rough Notes Taken During Some Rapid Journeys Across the Pampas and Among the Andes.* I loved the title, and the style, which performed his rushed journeys with dashes, half-finished phrases, and hasty impressions. This find gave me the idea that I could write my dissertation on nineteenth-century British travelers to Argentina. It would allow me to continue to be a Victorianist but also have a connection to a Spanish-speaking place.

As soon as I could get funding, I went to Buenos Aires. It was 2000, right before the financial crisis. Walking the leafy streets in the morning as the shopkeepers poured soapy water across their sidewalks reminded me so much of Barcelona, but without the discomfort of not being fluent in Catalan. Some of the zones of the city had obviously been planned with the same modernist sensibilities as Barcelona's Eixample neighborhood.

I liked the way *porteños* pronounced the *y* and the *ll* as *sh*, and I liked the conversations that I had with scholars, acquaintances, and people I met on the street. We were speaking Spanish, but the content was like nothing I had ever discussed with my family or their friends in Spain. Buenos Aires is a city steeped in psychoanalytic traditions and influences. People are comfortable talking about their narcissism, their hysterical compulsions, and their neurotic drives. Not only do they discuss these psychological issues on the individual level; they extend the analysis to the national predicament. I couldn't believe how self-aware they seemed, compared to the uptight, anti-therapy conversations I always had with my family in Spain, who insisted that you didn't need to talk endlessly about your problems.

I had never talked to anyone about psychoanalysis, and I had never had such introspective conversations *in Spanish*. Learning the vocabulary and the innuendos of how to talk about affect, emotion, and interrelationality in my mother tongue felt like a maturation that had been off limits to me.

The dissertation I ended up writing had a lot more to do with Argentina's literature and culture than with British culture. Yes, I read Darwin and Head and W.H. Hudson, but I was much more intrigued by the ways in which Domingo Sarmiento, Perito Moreno, Jorge Luis Borges, and Ricardo Piglia understood their national identity. They fashioned the Argentine self, both individual and collective, through reading the ways that the British portrayed their country and character.

What fascinated me in their writing were the ways in which they simultaneously seemed to say to the European elites who wrote about Argentina, "Tell me who I am," and "You have no idea who I am." Like them, I had spent my life saying, "I'm American! No, I'm Spanish. No, wait, I'm Latina. I'm New World. I'm Old World. See me, know me, but don't you dare try to pin me down."

Nobody

I kept wondering what Dr. O thought of me. I imagined that he had access to knowledge about what was wrong with me. He wasn't the first person onto whom I had projected this idea. There had been a long line of teachers, parents, siblings, lovers, and colleagues, who I believed understood my behaviors and gestures better than I could. They must be able to interpret everything that oozed out of me. I wanted them to tell me what they knew.

By putting Dr. O in these imagined authority roles, I was engaging in *transference*. Transference is the unconscious process by which you redirect your feelings from one person, often someone from your past, onto the analyst. It is a necessary part of the analysis because it allows both of you to begin to see the structures, feelings, and habits that shape you and your ways of being in the world.

Unconsciously, I imagined he was all those roles because they conferred an authority that would make him the person who knew — who really knew — something about me. That authority is what Jacques Lacan calls "the subject supposed to know."[13] Because I supposed him to know, I kept asking Dr. O questions, either implicitly or explicitly, like: Why do I act the way I do? Is what I'm doing true, or am I being manipulative? What can I do to make you love me? What am I? Who am I? What should I do?

Unlike all the other people who had attempted to give me answers to those questions and failed, he didn't answer. He just made me aware of how desperately I kept asking. For a long time, I didn't know how to stop. I kept falling back on the idea that someone out there knew the truth about me. It's how I grew up, believing in the authority of religion, or school, or older men. Even though I'd watched *The Wizard of Oz* and knew that there was no real power behind the curtain, I still believed that there was someone or something who knew better than I did what was good for me and what I needed. Whether it was a person or an institution (like church or state) or a structure (patriarchy, cultural norms, society), there was a "subject supposed to know" that acted as the "should" in my head. It was the authority that expected me to act in certain ways. Believing in its existence absolved me from having to ask harder questions about my responsibilities and commitments.

Transference was made easier by the fact that Dr. O and I never looked at each other. I lay on the couch, staring at the ceiling, the window, the painting in front of me. I listened to his quiet breathing. I heard him cough when he was sick. His pen scratched or he flipped through papers. I didn't really know what he looked like though. Even when I walked through the door every day, I looked down instead of catching his eye. Those kinds of embodied interactions always stayed awkward, because we never got to know each other the way two people who spent forty-five minutes a day together normally would.

Dr. O's job was to manage the counter-transference. He had to always remember that I was not talking to *him* when I said that I hated him or loved him or knew that he was judging me. He needed to be impervious to my demands and my seductions, so that we could both look at how they worked and what they stood in for.

Many times I assumed that he was bored. But more often than not, it was my own resistance that masqueraded as boredom. Other times, I told him that I was sure that the only reason that he continued to listen to me was that he was in love with me, that he wouldn't be interested otherwise. He said, "You want me to be like Odysseus who can withstand the siren's song?"

"How grandiose is that," I laughed, "that I think I'm irresistible?"

He didn't respond. Like he didn't respond to all the accusations. If he had given me anything back, I would have begun to hone my thoughts and responses in order to elicit a response from him. I would have become obsessed with our relationship, and repeated my usual patterns of giving myself and my desire away.

At times, I wasn't able to understand or see anything, so blinded was I by fear and rage. Like the Cyclops who has just lost his only eye, I demanded to know who he was that he could cause me this much pain. He, like Odysseus, would respond, "I'm nobody." In not asserting his own personality or wishes or judgments, he allowed me to project onto him whoever I needed him to be at that moment in the analysis.

Since he didn't, I had no choice but to stay true to the task of my psychoanalysis, which was to make the shift from believing in an imagined authority figure who would take what I gave him, to trusting my own obscure self-knowledge. That knowledge could emerge as long as he continued to be the nobody I needed him to be.

Women's World

I don't remember if I felt pleasure that night on the beach in Mallorca. Maybe I was turned on to have a secret with a powerful man that my family knew and trusted. Or maybe I faked it and convinced even myself, because, as I learned in later years, if you tell yourself you wanted a sexual encounter, then it doesn't feel like rape.

When my cousins and I returned to the *finca,* I didn't tell anyone what had happened with the pilot. A few days later, though, he called and asked me if I could meet him at the Reina Sofia Hotel during his overnight stopover. I hadn't imagined that it was something that could ever be spoken of or repeated, that he would actually want to turn it into something that we both chose to do. His assumption that I would want to continue made me feel complicit. I was in a situation I couldn't handle by myself.

Late in the kitchen after everyone had gone to bed, I told my godmother. She was of a different generation from my mother, almost half her age. I trusted that she, at least, wouldn't accuse me of having brought it on myself. I didn't know how to explain what had happened. I tripped over half-words until she asked, *¿te metió mano?* I had never heard the expression, literally translated as "did he put a hand inside you?" I figured it was close enough. In naming it, she labeled it an obvious transgression, something that he did to me. But if I told her what he had really done maybe I would have seemed more in the wrong. *Sí,* I said with relief, *me metió mano.*

My godmother told me that he, like so many airline pilots, was known to "have a woman in every port." That meant, I guess, that I hadn't caused him to fall; that he was already fallen. Or at least, that was the version that both she and I asserted to each other as we stood awkwardly at the counter. We couldn't bring ourselves to sit at the table because that would have meant that we were really going to talk about it. Neither of us was ready for that.

What I couldn't explain was that it gave me a frisson of excitement. Hadn't this man risked his marriage and his reputation to get a taste of me? Or maybe it hadn't been risky at all. Maybe he'd known that I was a bad girl, one who would rather be eaten out on a rock than be safely escorted back to her hotel. I must have shown that I wanted it, or he wouldn't have done it. My godmother treated me as if I was an innocent victim of inappropriate sexual advances. Perhaps, though, I was a desirous young woman who was guilty of misconduct.

I didn't mind her version of events. I wanted to be the good innocent girl who had become prey to a cheating womanizer. In the kitchen that night, it wasn't my fault that men wanted me. I was the victim of the perils of adult life. When she suggested that we not expose him for his wife's sake, I accepted. With a stroke of her fairy wand, my godmother had transformed me from a provocative slut into a wise generous girl who hid her abuse so as to not ruin another woman's life.

That evening I was inducted into a much more complicated women's landscape than I had understood when I flaunted my freedom in the face of their constraint. The mothers and aunts were not just judgmental uptight adults who couldn't enjoy themselves sexually or who policed my behavior towards the men who wanted me. They were also practical because they knew the tired score: men pursue young girls; men leave their wives; men get other wives. Better to let him have his *capricho* than to expose him.

Because chances are, the ones who suffer from the exposure are the women. The girl that the man pursues is shamed for inciting him. The wife is criticized (by other women mostly) for not pleasing her husband enough to keep him faithful. The prostitutes and mistresses that he visits are dismissed as necessary releases for his uncontrollable sexual needs. If a wife isn't willing to turn a blind eye towards her husband's philandering, she might end up on her own. Other women jump at the chance to get her newly divorced ex. There is no good outcome.

This women's world maintains its comforts and class privilege through a complicity with patriarchal norms. It is somberly realistic about the social realities that prioritize the man — no matter what his behavior — and punish the woman who complained or demanded too much.

The conversation wasn't enough for me. It couldn't be. Not when the words that we agreed upon to describe what had happened were untrue, standing in for something else that was still unspeakable. Not when I saw how much these women capitulated in order to maintain their standing. Not when I had already been introduced in America to the sex-positive optimism of that ubiquitous feminist book of the 1980s, *Our Bodies Ourselves*. Yes, I wanted to be a good girl, but at the same time I wanted those conservative Spanish women to be empowered and embrace their liberation.

Standing there in the kitchen, though, I glimpsed something about the inequality and power dynamics of sexual encounters, and the troubles that they caused. I was glad enough to be talked to as a woman by another woman. It wasn't much, but it was shelter in a community that disparaged the men who wielded power over them, and who shored up against victimhood through a ladylike decorum of their own.

Fridays

For the first six months, I went to analysis four days a week. The rhythm of it had become very recognizable: Friday to Sunday, I immersed myself in home and family and friends and work. I didn't think about analysis or the images and ideas that emerged in it. Sunday night I slept badly with vivid disturbing dreams. Mondays I felt dread at reimmersion and walked there with a pit in my stomach. Tuesday and Wednesday I delved deeper into what emerged, often crying or having physical symptoms of fear. On Thursday, though, thoughts began to grind to halting stops. In the middle of working through a painful and slowly emerging idea or memory, I would mutter abruptly, "What does it matter anyway?" and go silent. It was like a dam that shut off the flowing current of the unconscious, sealing it in anticipation of the three-day separation.

One Thursday, I pointed this pattern out.

Dr. O said, "We could meet on Fridays as well."

I hadn't known it was even possible. That weekend, I obsessed about it. Did he think that I could afford even more time to lie on his couch? I was already taking an hour and a half out of my four workdays to commute and lie there. I was a busy woman, and I didn't need that much analysis, did I?

Monday through Wednesday of that week I was very articulate in my different reactions as I cycled through all the trouble he had stirred up in me with that offer. In rapid succession, I said things like,

"You really fucked up asking to see me more. Why would you?"

"You think I'm completely damaged and crazy and that you need to watch over me more closely."

"You don't usually work on Fridays, so you're making an exception for me because you're in love with me and want to see me more. This is a trap. You're a captor and I won't be your captive."

"Your offer is like a gingerbread house, which lures me because it seems like a house of plenty, but I should be on my guard since it has more sinister motives. You will consume me."

"You are ill and you have a devouring need for me. You will want to see me more and more and then you will die."

Dr. O didn't respond. I became more shrill as I blamed him for his misstep. He listened. I ran out of accusations and began to listen as well. I heard my accusations, recriminations, projections, and spirals of paranoia. They seemed to loop on endless repeat in the back of my head or in the pit of my gut. Underneath their noise, I could also hear a constant murmur of fear and desire.

All of a sudden, my resistance collapsed. I had, after all, been the one to bring up the idea of more continuity. But when I was given what I had half-asked for, the half that hadn't freaked out. I was scared that he had acceded. Most men gave me what I said I wanted, but I distrusted both my requests and their motives. I couldn't trust that he had said yes because he deemed my demand legitimate. I worried that he was seduced by me.

Try as I might to discern his motives, they were irrelevant. What mattered was that I begin to know what I wanted. That was the harder task.

"It's so much easier," I said, "to shape myself to other people's desires for me. I want what they want me to want."

"Once upon a time, said Dr. O, "there was a baby girl whose face formed, but she found it was so malleable that it could become whatever the other wanted or needed."

It sounded like he was asking me to embrace my inner child. But I knew that Dr. O wasn't a self-help kind of therapist. He wasn't asking me to develop an affirmative mantra that would deflect the power that others had over me. Instead, the strict boundaries of our relationship were revealing the malleability of my borders.

My previous *modus operandi* had been to ask other people implicit forms of the question, "Who do you think I am?" Whatever I thought they thought I was, I would be that. In the analysis, though, I was in a relationship in which he refused to answer the question. He wouldn't rise to the bait, though I tried in various ways. He didn't try to convince me or give me advice. To the best of his ability, he didn't impose his own ideas about attractive women, or unhappy wives, or highly educated professors, or whatever else he saw in me. He gave me back not what he thought of me, but what he heard me saying.

Psychoanalysis is called the talking cure. That doesn't mean talking to yourself. It means a conversation. It's a dialectic in which each of the parties learns from the other's viewpoint. A new truth emerges from the contradictions. I didn't actually need his phone number way back at the beginning. But now I was requesting something that I did need: more continuity to be able to do the work of analysis. Able to finally quiet all the accusatory narratives that were crowding my mind, I claimed the Friday as something I wanted.

"What Does a Woman Want?"

Since I was a teenager, I had rape dreams. One that recurred: I am driving with an older man. I sit in the passenger seat and he asks me to shift the gears for him. I make a show of fondling the stick, unaware of why I am eroticizing it, if I'm actually turned on or just performing it. Even though he's asked me to share control, he is the one deciding what we're doing and where we're going. As we drive through the beautiful countryside, he says he wants to show me something because I'm special. He turns the car down a narrow road but it leads into a dark basement. He holds up a thick black cord. I say, "No, you don't have to do this. I want to. Don't rape me." I kiss him and surprise myself with a groan of desire as I feel his warm soft skin. I try to sweet-talk and touch my way out of it, but he just holds up the black cord again. I don't understand why it has to be this way, when I've already given myself willingly.

I said to Dr. O, "I don't want you to think that I have rape fantasies."

"You don't want me to take the dreams at face value?"

I thought for awhile. "Yes, that's it. I don't want you or me to pin these dreams down through an obvious interpretation, because it'll get us stuck. If I continue to free associate, maybe we'll get somewhere else." The dreams had such a circular logic: I want to have power over the man by making him desire me. His desire is to wield his power over me. So then the only power I have is to proactively want sex so as to divest him of his power. I felt like this was more to it than just a fantasy of loss of power.

Over the months of talking to Dr. O, I began to recall late-night situations in hotels and dorm rooms. Me, speaking too fast, laughing too hard, leaning in towards an older man who I had spent the evening talking to over a conference dinner or an academic event. My face flushed and my eyes bright. Drunk, but still drinking. Adrenaline pumping, dread and desire in my gut, I'd break the tension by initiating, giving myself over to the situation with gusto. If I took the reins, then I was an empowered woman who was liberated enough to share her body openly with men. I did like the sex. It was the mounting inevitability before it that I hated. The sick feeling of having no choice.

"I remember a man I knew in Buenos Aires. He wanted to have sex. For once, I actually refused even though I felt like he expected it. He told me I was *una histérica*. For years, I would say to people, 'Can you believe how sexist this guy was? Just because I wouldn't fuck him he pathologized me! Same old tired history of diagnosing women as hysterics when they're sick, or volatile, or seen to be attention-seeking.'"

I still didn't accept that guy's lay diagnosis. But I was starting to get what hysteria means in psychoanalytic terms. Hysteria is a structure in which your desire is shaped in response to another's demand. You don't desire the man so much as the image of yourself being desired by him. I had often been turned on by being the object of a man's uncontrollable desire. So when I asked Dr. O to hold off on an easy interpretation of the rape dreams, I was intuiting that we could get closer to discovering the place from which I desired. In other words, the subject with whom I identified: the man, the powerful man. I wanted what he wanted.

Freud seemed so reductive and patronizing when he asked that infamous question: "What does a woman want?" There's merit to the question, though, or at least it felt like there was as I asked "What do *I* want?" As a heterosexual woman, shaped by a family and society in which men have an inordinate share of the power, I was trying to figure out what desires were available to me. According to Lacan, the fundamental hysterical question is "Am I a man or am I a woman?"[14] I took this to mean: which one am I when I desire?

That question, I realized on the couch, has always been constitutive for me. The boy next door and I used to play that we were brothers, skilled swordsmen or intrepid sailors or courageous outlaws. I cut my hair short so that adults would see us together and call us "young men." I even peed standing up. I only played with dolls in the secrecy of my room, because I didn't want anyone to know that I was that soft or feminine. As I grew older, I had elaborate erotic fantasies about a group of women preparing a woman for a man's pleasure. What I was trying to figure out in analysis now was whether I was I turned on by imagining I was the woman being done, or the man doing.

The recurring dreams delved into what I knew without knowing, and without wanting to know. Power wasn't something I could just claim for myself, despite my intellect or my attempts at self-empowerment. It was a structural condition that molded my desires. Much as I fondled the clutch or got turned on by a kiss, I was a woman in a man's world. The lure that I threw out playfully was replaced by the thick cord that has been there all along. That cord emerged, in the analysis, as a symbol of this unconscious conflict and its brutal enactment.

Entrapment

I never saw Dr. O use the bathroom in the waiting room. I, on the other hand, used it almost every time I had a session, either before or after, to pee or sob or empty my cramping gut or wipe my smudged eye makeup. It had a shower in it that was never used. Sometimes it housed a fragile tall plant that seemed to tremble under its overhead light. When I felt most trapped and angry at having to undergo this dreadful process, I would gaze through the shower glass at the willowy plant. She and I were captive to this man, who hoarded us down there with him in the gloom of the underground.

One spring I noticed she was gone. I couldn't stop thinking about her. I worried that she had died and been thrown away. Finally, I blurted out, at the end of the session,

"What happened to the plant in the shower? Did you kill it?"

I think he had been about to say "and that's our time for today," but realized that I really needed to know. "The plant is outside, and healthy because of having been sheltered indoors through the cold winter."

I was relieved at the answer and that he had answered me. The relief didn't last long, however, because, upon second thought, I perceived sympathy in his response. This perturbed the balance that I liked him to maintain. I wanted him to demonstrate, continuously and without fail, that he was not capitulating to me. When I cried and shook in front of him, I worried that I was exposing myself to effect. Perhaps my tears weren't genuine. Perhaps they were just a ploy that I was using to hook him in. So if he seemed to reassure me, I got angry that he was being gullible.

It was quite a spiral. At one point of it I'd begin to work myself into anger over his stupid male susceptibility to my wiles.

Then I would realize that he wasn't falling for me. He wasn't going to be nice and let me stop doing this painful work of speaking. That would make me hit the point in the spiral in which I feared that he was a collector, a man who would take advantage of his power and my trust by cutting me off from the outside world. He was going to trap me so as to keep me close.

My father–daughter incest fantasies and fears reemerged in one of the turns of this cycle. Echoing the story of enthrallment with which I started the analysis, I began talking with fascinated fear about the Austrian Josef Fritzl, who imprisoned his daughter in his cellar for twenty-four years. Fritzl attempted to defend himself by saying that he was trying to stop her from doing drugs or having sex.

I couldn't stop imagining what her life must have been. Trapped in the basement, she would have waited anxiously for him, her only bearer of food and supplies, knowing that if he did not return, she and her children/siblings would be trapped without possibility of rescue. At the same time, she would have dreaded the footsteps of her jailer, rapist, and father.

I, too, felt trapped by a cruel authority figure who demanded I delve into the darkness of the basement! And he, too, reassured me that he would be constant, and help me manage life down there! I knew I was exaggerating, but my panic was palpable as I drew the similarities between Fritzl and Dr. O.

"The children in my psyche fear that we'll be forgotten. That you'll stop coming and leave us locked up. But, at the same time, I desperately want you to leave me alone, to just stop making me be here with you."

"Ah... Brer Rabbit."

I was startled. Dr. O didn't often offer a free association of his own.

He continued, "When Brer Rabbit begs to not be thrown in the briar patch, he's playing at not wanting to be released into the place where he will be most comfortable and safe."

I thought for awhile, then said, "So it's like when I beg you not to fall for me — 'don't love me so much that you want me all for your very own.' I fear your love or care because I insist it will smother me, break me down, or break me open. But you're saying I'm like Brer Rabbit, because what I actually want is for you to care for me and make me feel safe. So maybe I am actually asking you to hoard me, smother me, keep me in a constrained place that I will be able to break open or break down."

The next day I came in, unable to shake the memory of Fritzl's daughter, of Brer Rabbit's pleas. I said, "Here is what it has been like for me. I've talked, flirted, and been open with a man. The encounter leads towards sex. I have to. I'm trapped. I've gotten myself into this. So I fake wanting it. It's a way to stay smooth, to not expose a fault line that could break me apart. It's rape. Maybe I don't admit it, and he doesn't know it, but it is rape. Because I don't want to be there. I'm nervous. I'm out of control."

I felt like I was going to throw up. I muttered, "I hate them, those stupid fuckers, for thinking we had a good time. I hate myself, for trying to think of it as yet another sexual exploit."

Dr. O was silent for a long time, and then said, "Fault line?"

I too was silent for minutes. And then I began to speak as if I were recounting a dream. One time David and I hiked in a forest in California. The thick moss that covered the ground gave a spring to our steps. We looked over at a line of tall ferns that had wisps of steam surrounding them. When we went closer and peered down at the ground between the plants, the heat hit our faces. We were standing on a fault line, looking down into the red and orange embers of the insides of the earth itself. It scared the fuck out of me to see the danger that lay below the soft cool ground on which I was standing.

I started to shake. "What does it even feel like, to penetrate? To push a pulsing part of your own body into the warm interior of another person? I allowed those men inside me. That's what we straight women do. We get penetrated. We fuck, we receive, we take in. I'm so compliant I even come when I get penetrated."

I knew that I didn't usually think of sex in this way. I didn't know why I was saying this. I was so angry, so aggressive towards Dr. O as those burning words flowed out of me.

"How do I know I even wanted to be analyzed? Maybe I just agreed to it because I felt trapped by your male authority. What if I have just fallen into another relationship with a man that reenacts this fucked up father-daughter shit?"

He was silent. My sobs subsided. I became silent too. Our listening penetrated deep into the boiling emotions that lay below my smooth exterior.

Splitting

At parties, David would watch me from across the room as I laughed and confided and listened attentively in a group. On our way home, he would say, "You really hit it off with those people!"

I'd roll my eyes, "Them? What insufferable bores!"

Since he was unable to fake it in social situations, he found this to be, at first, an interesting twist of my personality, and later, proof of my inauthenticity and dishonesty.

I would say, "I don't know, it's just what you do, you give the other person what they want in order to get through the evening."

Even my switch from first person to second with the use of "you" shows how accustomed I was to splitting myself. I thought of it as commonplace social behavior. "Take her, she's yours" wasn't just something that had been done to me, but something that I did routinely.

Talking about this to Dr. O, I remembered a miniature porcelain duck family that I had as a child. The mother and one of the ducklings swam on the surface of the blue china pond, but the third one gave the illusion of diving since it was just a tail and little webbed feet. As I described it, Dr. O referred to a poem called "Autotomy" by Wisława Szymborska, about a sea creature that protects itself through a self-imposed mutilation. The second I got home I looked it up:

> In danger, the holothurian cuts itself in two.
> It abandons one self to a hungry world
> and with the other self it flees.[15]

I saw why Dr. O had thought of it. Like my duckling — "Take my cute little ass, it's yours!" — the sea cucumber splits itself. It must feel really threatened to divide in such a way, jettisoning a part of itself in order to survive. I recognized that strange and desperate instinct to give a part of yourself away so as to preserve another untouched. You have to numb and cauterize the place where the split is made, creating partitions and compartments that seal off the jettisoned parts. When my little girl fingers picked up the duckling's tail and turned it over, there was nothing, just raw unpainted porcelain and a hole that exposed its emptiness. But when it sat on the surface of the pond, it looked so convincingly whole, just partly hidden in the depths.

The next day, I said, "So in exposing what seemed too intimate, in giving strangers my attention or my love or my ass, was I keeping my head below the surface? Or was my head up my ass?"

"Head up your ass?"

I laughed, "That's what I yell at David when we're fighting: 'Get your head out of your ass!' He just seems so oblivious, so self-absorbed, so narcissistic."

I didn't often talk about David. All that energy and time that Wendy and I had spent dissecting my marriage felt like lost time that I couldn't get back. Without having planned it, I was excluding David from the space of the analysis so that I could talk about other things.

Or maybe Dr. O was engineering David's exclusion. When I brought David up, it seemed that he would bring the associations back to me. Like his response that day, "What about you? Is your head hidden in an intimate and fantastical space inside of you?"

I said, "It does feel like I have a compartment within me. Where I can keep my thoughts and fantasies hidden from view. From the outside, it still seems like I'm exposing myself for other people's consumption and enjoyment, but there's that secret space that no one can see."

In our various returns to the scene of "take her, she's yours," Dr. O and I were formulating an idea of why I split myself. It was obviously a coping strategy that I learned early in life due to the split of two mothers, two classes, three — Spanish, American, Salvadorean — cultures.

That wasn't the only interpretation though. Analysis was always about telling a story, and retelling it, and reinterpreting it. The more I thought about splitting, the more connections I made. I began to put into words other versions, other pieces of evidence that pointed to a larger systemic need to split. Inextricable from the earlier family structure that I'd inhabited were the sexual politics that surrounded me in our culture, and the intimate effects they had on my sense of self. It didn't feel safe out there, in the sea of men.

Maybe I split myself because I learned, as a young girl, to give bits away, and to hide away those that seemed unattractive or repulsive. Or maybe because the men broke bits of me off for consumption. They devoured me with their eyes or hands. These men were so unaware of the ways that they dismembered women. They were drawn to a flash of leg or a flutter of eyelash or a witty turn of phrase. Their eyes unconsciously landed on a piece of body, and we women noticed. I got this queasy thrill of repulsion and excitement when I saw the power that a part of me had over a man, if he was more aroused by legs or by cleavage, by gestures or by a certain kind of smile. Once I knew what attracted him to me, I gave it to him.

I was matter-of-fact as I spoke about this to Dr. O. I wanted him to know the ways that men fetishize and objectify women from a young age. Maybe I wanted him to acknowledge his own collusion in the way that men look at women. Or maybe I wanted to know if he wanted a piece of me, so that I could give it to him. I sometimes felt him look at me as I lay on the couch, but I never sensed his eyes fixating on my body. I couldn't tell if he was attracted to my mind either. There was nothing I could offer that I knew would hit the mark for him.

"Other times," I said, "it's something about my personality. One man may be turned on by assertiveness and intelligence, while another gets aroused by naiveté and insecurity. I am all of those, so I can just segment parts of myself for him. It doesn't feel like faking. It's an accentuation of some personal qualities and a muting of others. I play with foregrounding and concealing. I share what I think is his object of desire. And I hide the rest away."

I went home and did keyword searches — "splitting," "division," "half" — on the digitized *Collected Works of Freud* that I had downloaded on my computer. I found what sounded like the same instinct that the holothurian enacts. According to Freud, the ego avoids "a rupture in any direction by deforming itself, by submitting to encroachments on its own unity and even perhaps by effecting a cleavage or division of itself."[16] To protect its unity, in other words, it splits itself. What a pained logic that chooses the breaking off of parts over the risk of attack to the vulnerable self. It's safer, I guessed, to do it yourself. At least that way you can choose where the split occurs.

Deserving

Dr. O and I were entering into the second year of the analysis. I was so sick of talking about men and seduction and power. Over and over again, I heard echoes of my mother's, "What do you do to men?" which led me to keep asking, "Am I the one doing something, or are they? Do I want them, or do I want what they want?"

What I was starting to see was that these were the wrong questions, because they were directed towards Dr. O as hysterical demands. On a fundamental level, I kept asking him to tell me if I was inherently lovable, or just someone who tricked people into loving her. Was I a passive victim or an active agent? He never answered. Any answer he could have given would only lead to dissatisfaction on my part.

When I commented on this, he said, "Hysteria is a hard one. The questions depend on what the fish is looking for."

Wait what? The fish? Was he implying that I was using the questions I posed to him as lures to hook him? That would mean that I only asked the questions that I thought he wanted to answer. That I didn't even know what questions I really wanted to ask about myself.

Sometimes when I ask a friend for advice, I'll say, "Don't just answer what you think I want to hear." Dr. O's version of this would be the opposite: "Don't just ask the questions that you think I want to answer."

My questions to him functioned as offerings. Here you go, wise man, here's my question. You can answer and advise me, which will make you like how I made you feel wise. You'll want me to ask you more, and I will, because I will like that I've hooked you. But I'll never be satisfied because they're the wrong answers to the wrong questions.

Dr. O used the metaphor of men as fish. As we talked, I free associated to another marine creature: the siren whose seductive song lures men towards the dangerous cliffs where they will perish. Her desire isn't an innocent yearning for the men's company, but rather a power struggle to undo them. She swims in her domain, and destroys the men who imagine they are easily sailing over it.

In one of his more disturbing essays, Freud talks about the dangers of transference and countertransference.[17] It may be difficult, he warns, for a doctor to refuse his female patient who imagines that she is in love with him. After all, "there is an incomparable fascination in a woman of high principles who confesses her passion."[18] The doctor must resist, much as the sailor's must resist the siren's radiant magic. The patient, Freud warns, is dangerous, since she will "try to make him captive to [her] socially untamed passion." The doctor must not allow himself to be captivated, because he should understand that she is just engaged in transference.

"When I ask you all these questions, it's as if," I said to Dr. O, "I'm crying out 'Have me!' Which sounds like 'Halve me!' Take the half that I tantalizingly put before you and that way we can both forget about the contradictory elements, the ways in which seduction may be destruction, knowledge may be ignorance."

"Take either your human torso or your fish tail?"

"Yes, but don't try to make me acknowledge that I am both woman and fish!"

I laughed at my joke, but then felt embarrassed. "I'm a feminist!" I said. "How can it be that I am comparing myself to a siren? Like I'm some kind of stereotypical femme fatale."

"Should you be in control of all your actions? Your impulses and attractions?"

"I don't know. There have certainly been times when my flirtation has gotten me into trouble. I should have known better. Blegh. I feel so guilty for my behavior."

Dr. O didn't bite at the self-blame I dangled in front of him. Instead, he said, "Having an unconscious is not a moral failing."

Having an unconscious is not a moral failing. It still sends shivers down my spine. If I accepted this, I could put a stop to the vicious circle of trying to figure out who deserved what, who was to blame. I could, instead, understand that we all act on unconscious impulses. None of us fully understand our own intentions and fears and desires. That's the weird thing about how we act in the world: we expect each other to be self-aware and conscious of our actions, yet so much of the time we're projecting strange fantasies and demands of which we aren't even aware.

I had expected him to chastise me or to be turned on by me. When he did neither, I said, "I look forward to seeing what a man does with a hysteric if he doesn't slap her or fuck her, the way that doctors did to them throughout history."

"It seems," he said, "that she's waiting for something to be done to her."

I was. I was waiting for him to do to me what I deserved. Wasn't that what life was like, a system of rewards and punishments? I began to hear that I often used commonplace expressions such as "That's so unfair," or "I earned this," or "I must have done something to deserve this." I remembered a line that David had read aloud to me from Ursula Le Guin's *The Dispossessed*:

> For we each of us deserve everything, every luxury that was ever piled in the tombs of the dead kings, and we each of us deserve nothing, not a mouthful of bread in hunger. Have we not eaten while another starved? Will you punish us for that? Will you reward us for the virtue of starving while others ate? No man earns punishment, no man earns reward. Free your mind of the idea of deserving, the idea of earning, and you will begin to be able to think.[19]

Each of us deserve everything… each of us deserve nothing. This idea eschews a moral universe in which someone or something *knows* what we deserve. Maybe we desperately want to believe that a tally is being kept, even if we chafe at the idea of being judged. Or maybe, as the quotation suggests, we believe that there is such a system because it unburdens us of the task of having to think.

My mother may have blamed me for whatever it was I "did to men," but I was no powerful siren nor a conniving witch. I was a woman with an attractive body, heterosexual desire, fear of rejection, and a history of having been given away. That is more than enough to do something to narcissistic men who get off on protecting, saving, or fucking pretty girls. Maybe we were all acting through patterns that we didn't understand or recognize, both because they were too deep inside us and too large outside of us.

PART TWO

Thus she acted out an essential part of her recollections and phantasies instead of reproducing them in the treatment.

— Freud, "Dora"

PART TWO

PART TWO

Catch Me

When I was 20, I started rock climbing. It was when I was doing my Masters in Critical and Cultural Theory in Wales. I guess it served as an antidote to the awkward and somewhat posturing days that I spent with the theory crowd, talking about French philosophy or deconstruction. With the climbers, I was the only girl in a sea of eager men who watched from below as I swarmed up the coastal cliffs. The sharp limestone rocks shredded my fingertips. I felt no fear as I looked at the crashing waves below. It was easy to not think, to be in my body, no matter how dangerous or painful the situation. It gave me a clarity of purpose I didn't usually have.

In the evenings the group went to the pub. The otherwise dour and shy men would get drunk and increasingly loud as they mimed overhang grips and tenuous handhold hooks. Sometimes one of them would walk me home. Alan, a wiry Scotsman, was my regular escort. He was an excellent climber and an appreciative lover who quivered with arousal as he touched me with his nimble climbing fingers. It was clear that he was getting something from me that he wasn't getting from his live-in girlfriend.

David was in Canada. He was my confidante, my best friend, my lover. He knew about the climbers, and claimed to feel no jealousy. When he came to visit, I insisted we go to the Pembroke sea cliffs, even though he suffered from fear of heights. I climbed as he tried his hand at belaying me from below. Alan gave him some tips. Halfway up, I called down to ask my future husband if he was paying attention. He didn't answer, so I jumped off the rock face. I swung fifteen feet out through the air as he braked the rope correctly and caught me. Both men were furious that I had done that to a novice.

When I told Dr. O the story of the cliff jump, he said, "A dangerous move, indeed."

As a practiced climber, I knew better. It was reckless. I wanted to make sure he was paying attention. Could he hold onto me, even though I was promiscuous and impulsive? Would he give me some slack but pull tight if I was falling?

"Would he," I said to Dr. O, "always catch me?"

De Man

I was talking about David in the analysis. I guess I had tested the waters for over a year and seen that I could delve into the dangerous depths of the marriage. In the weeks that followed, I began to tell more and more of the story of our relationship.

McGill University library, 1988. I was nineteen. He was a twenty-nine-year old returning student who had spent years being a missionary, housepainter, gravedigger, and a lapsed evangelical Christian. David was the golden boy of the English department because of his lyrical prose, earnest diatribes, and meandering brilliance. He was beautiful, exuding radiant health from his long lean body and shaggy hair. When I first saw him walk into the graduate seminar on Samuel Richardson's *Clarissa*, I thought, "Who's this Marlboro Man? Not my type, but still...."

On a snowy January afternoon, I sat at my carrel trying to read deconstructionist critic Paul de Man's "Rhetoric of Temporality" for my Literary Theory seminar. David wandered by, wearing the yellow rubber pants and construction boots that he used for winter cycling. I told him I couldn't make sense of the essay. He stripped down to his long johns and sat next to me, his thigh hot. The smell of his armpits reminded me of the irresistible taste of gnawing on wooden pencils in grade school. Hours passed as we worked through the essay, sentence-by-sentence.

What we understood, once we muddled past the analysis of Romantic poetry, was that de Man was arguing against a false synthesis of subject and object. To strive for unity between self and other was an illusion. Instead—and this is what excited us almost as much as our physical proximity—de Man talked about a language and an ethics that "prevents the self from an illusory identification with the non-self, which is now fully, though painfully, recognized as a non-self."[20] Aroused by intellectual excitement and bodily chemistry, we immediately took this from the realm of literary criticism to our own lives. It was the key to our problems, we told each other, describing past and present relationships in which we mistakenly imagined the possibility of union with our lover. Instead, we now understood, one is always at a distance from others, and from oneself. The demand for romantic union hurt because it was a mistaken way of imagining self and other. This new idea was a perfect segue to our intimate confessions of previous heartbreaks and sentimental woes.

At that time, I was in a long-distance relationship with Martin, a much older professor whom I had met at the end of an Oxford study program. We slept together the night we first talked to each other, despite the fact that I was dating one of his students that summer. Neither of us seemed to consider the pain it would cause him. Our getting together also caused concern from some of the other instructors, who tried to warn me about him, alluding to a history of violence with a prior staff member, that, because it was so veiled, didn't make much sense to me. I ignored them, refusing to think there was anything wrong with a thirty-three-year-old man falling in love with a teenager. I was just more mature than most women my age, and plus, I did something to men.

Unexpectedly, he followed me to Spain only a week after I left Oxford. It was romantically impulsive, though strange for my family who didn't quite know how to behave around this professor who was so obviously obsessed with me. When I got back to

Montreal, he again showed up only two weeks later, surprising me and my roommate. I didn't think to ask how this seemed to his ex-wife, who was taking care of his young children while he spent his money chasing after me.

That semester, we wrote every day, talked on the phone often, and made plans to visit each other. He assumed I would move to Aberdeen to live with him as soon as I graudated. He even patted my belly at one point and talked about having children together. I felt certain I was in love, but couldn't quite imagine what I would do there, since my plans were to become a professor myself. I wasn't going to be the kind of professor that he was, either, with his boring biographical investigations of Joseph Conrad and Thomas Hardy, two writers that I had never liked. I was going to be a critical theorist.

The fall that I met David, I was insomniac and having very dark, despairing thoughts, though I couldn't admit to myself that I was feeling trapped by Martin and his vision of us. I thought I was just tormented by love. David was sweet and I confided in him as a friend, never thinking of him as a rival to the distinguished professor who occupied my heart and mind. Until, that is, the night David took me ice-skating on the frozen pond of Parc Lafontaine. I tottered out on my weak ankles. He glided effortlessly towards me across the ice, a swan swooping down to steady a wobbly duckling. Up until that moment, he had been a bit of a clown, seemingly naïve about life and eager to learn from me and with me. Now, though, I saw a different person, full of strength and confidence.

Over the years that followed, I came to distance myself from de Man, whose fascination with Romantic poetry was very far from my own interests in film, psychoanalysis, and feminism. I didn't stop reading him for the reason that many others did, which was the discovery of his wartime writings. As a young man in Nazi-occupied Belgium, de Man wrote some anti-Semitic newspaper articles. They were not discovered till after his death, and served, in many people's eyes, to discredit everything he had written subsequently. I wonder if he, a young ambitious intellectual, had felt trapped under the Nazis. Maybe he was blinded by that desire for power and recognition. Maybe he was pressured, even unconsciously, by his family. It seems to me that the shame of what he had done as a young man shaped his subsequent work. His pained acknowledgment of self-division and distance was the product of a rigorous intellectual examination of a life lived, decisions made. His work, in my mind, is written by someone who was trying to understand and repair the mistakes of his youth.

Reading that 1969 essay in 1988 was the moment I discovered I had a question. I wanted to know how to understand myself in relation to history, to politics, and to others. It's fitting that I developed that question with David, who seemed so different from the other men I encountered. And even more fitting that he ended up trapped with me in a fantasy of romantic love, despite our belief that we could transcend it if we just paid enough attention to the theoretical ideas that we were reading together.

Holding

It surprised me how much Dr. O and I turned to myth and fairytale. Rapunzel, Brer Rabbit, selkie, and siren seemed to be touchstones to which we circled back again and again. I wished I was a visual artist, so that I could draw the magical bestiary that populated my imagination. Included in it would be contemporary creatures as well, since I often brought up the voraciousness of Shrek, or No-Face in Miyazaki's *Spirited Away,* or Homer Simpson. These characters, who I knew so well from repeated watching with the kids, jostled in my mind as I talked about who deserved love, how you win love, when you are too hungry for love.

Another character that emerged for me was Jack Jack, the surprising baby from *The Incredibles.* Unlike the rest of his family, Jack Jack seems to have no superpowers. Left behind with the babysitter, he begins to exhibit startling traits. When the villain kidnaps him and attempts to fly away, Jack Jack's powers are unleashed. He rapidly transforms from baby to devil, from a ball of fire to a vicious robot. His name embodies his superpower, because Jack doubled is still Jack, whether he looks like a baby or a monster.

I wanted to have that power myself, to be able to hold and embody all the fiercely contradictory oppositions that seemed to reside within me, instead of splitting them off through dissociation, repression, or denial. It reminded me of Dylan Thomas's description in a letter to a friend: "I hold a beast, an angel, and a madman in me, and my enquiry is as to their working, and my problem is their subjugation and victory, downthrow and upheaval, and my effort is their self-expression."[21] In his poetry, Thomas sought to know and hold all those opposing manifestations by bringing them into language.

I, too, was engaged in an enquiry, a problem, and an effort. If I wanted to be less split and scared, I had to hold the range of contradictions. All of Jack Jack — biting, burning, screaming, cooing, cuddling, sleeping — needs to be held. The villain can't do it, and drops the raging baby, but his mother comes to his rescue, stretching herself wide to cradle him and slow his fall. It's a Pixar animation of Winnicott's "holding environment," in which the good-enough mother creates a feeling of safety in which the child can experience conflicting emotions and desires.[22]

In analysis, I kept having doubt about whether Dr. O was the villain who was trying to capture me but would be unable to hold me, or the mother who would catch me if I fell. Like Jack Jack, I manifested different characters and attributes — demon creature, changeling, ugly duckling, abandoned girl, siren, rape victim, good mother, loving wife, Little Red Riding Hood, Rapunzel, and Brer Rabbit. To hold them seemed impossible, yet also urgently necessary. What I didn't really understand was that they had emerged because I already was in a holding environment that was capacious enough for them all.

Psychoanalysis was holding me through its formal elements of punctuality, predictability, and objective impersonal listening. Dr. O and I were there so dependably every day that I came to trust that I would not be abandoned, no matter what parts of myself reared their ugly heads. In this space, I could admit that when I loved, I also hated; that when I was scared I was also attracted; that a desire to seduce could also be a desire to destroy. Neither of us demanded that I clarify or stick to one version. Instead, we attended to these oppositions, so that contradictory feelings, beliefs, and statements could be held without judgment or interpretation.

The way I'm writing about splitting and holding may sound as if I thought there was a unified self, a whole duckling, that I was supposed to become. If that was the case, it would be contradicting everything I had learned over the years of reading critical theories of subjectivity. Ever since reading that de Man essay, I knew that we perform parts of ourselves in different contexts, that the idea of a coherent self is illusory. To imagine anything else is to be like Peter Pan, attempting to sew his shadow back on so as to unify all the parts of himself, even the ones that are darkest and most unpredictable. I believed that we can never be self-same, that there's always a shadow trapped in a drawer or prancing around the room just out of hand's reach.

Did Dr. O know this? Or was I more well-read and theoretically sophisticated than he was? That's one of the problems of being an academic in psychoanalysis, that you always suspect that you've read more than your shrink has. We never talked about his training, or his intellectual formation, and I wondered if he had a more essentialist idea of what the self was. I feared that his goal for the psychoanalysis was not dissimilar to Wendy's: that I become complete unto myself, and transparent to myself and others. I could never bring myself to just ask him, however, because I was scared that he may sound reductive or stupid.

Projecting these ideas onto him, I turned him into some kind of superego that demanded self-coherence and unity. It wasn't just that. When I imagined that he believed that the opposite of splitting was wholeness, what I wasn't considering was where that idea had come from in the first place. What I mean is that Dr. O basically only worked with the words that I gave him. He would give them back so that I could hear them. He seldom offered his own thoughts on the subject, for which I was glad. I knew that if he'd been prescriptive, I would have tried to follow his suggestions to the letter, and then been furious at him if I failed to fulfill them. So, knowing that he mostly just echoed me, I had to wonder if the things he said about a whole self came from me, not him.

Despite all my theoretical knowledge about fragmented subjectivity, I still couldn't help but think of myself as a unified self. I used metaphors of interiority, as if there is an inside where emotion and thought reside. I clung to a continuity of my own history, and tried to attend to the primal and unresolved needs of the hurt scared small child that I was. I believed that there was some secret part of me, too vulnerable, too unattractive to be shown to others.

It's not so strange that it was hard to practice, in every day life, what I knew on a theoretical level. Our culture, after all, affirms a self that knows what it wants and says what it means. Our language is filled with ideas about self-knowledge that assume an inside, a depth, an inner wisdom, a movement towards "knowing oneself." In fact, it has become a responsibility. Motivational discourse tells us to be empowered and entrepreneurial versions of ourselves. There is little room in our legal, political, educational, or affective systems to be confused or driven by contradictory desires. We're supposed to know our minds.

However, we are made up of complex histories and ideologies that inform us in ways that we can only ever partially understand. The feminist Rosalind Gill talks about the pressures that our society puts on us to perform ourselves as "an overly rational and overly unified view of the self, with no space for fantasy, desire or unconscious investments, for splits or contradictions."[23] There is so much that we don't know about why we act the way we do, why we we cling so ardently to certain beliefs. In analysis, I was beginning to recognize how exhausted I was by my desperate attempts to compartmentalize the disparate codes that shaped me. I knew that my task was to hold the baby, no matter what other creatures emerged.

Monogamy

David and I didn't have sex the night we went skating. I was still involved with Martin. David insisted that he would not cheat on him. I didn't understand why it would affect Martin at all, given that he was faraway in Scotland.

Both David and Martin saw it differently. Back in September, when Martin and I were about to separate for the semester, I suggested that we see other people. He got furious with me, his face turning red with jealous anger. I quickly rescinded, saying that of course I was just speaking hypothetically, and that I couldn't imagine being attracted to anyone else.

But I could.

I was attracted to so many men! The freedom to sleep with whoever I wanted, whenever I wanted, was an inviolable right that I, as a feminist, would not give up. It was in keeping with my belief that everybody should have a lot of sex, that we all loved doing it and it shouldn't be limited. Martin had slept with me the first night he met me. Didn't that prove that he was not opposed to casual sex?

David's refusal was differently couched though. It wasn't about possession and monogamy; it was about honesty. He said he would sleep with me if I told Martin and he was okay with it. I knew from that terrifying outburst that there was no way Martin would agree. So I had to make a decision between the two. It was hard, because Martin sensed that he was losing me and tried to rein me in tightly. I didn't know, he insisted, how good our relationship was for both of us. When I graduated, we would marry. Considering I had just turned twenty, every word he said creeped me out more.

Finally, I allowed him to come to Montreal to argue his case in person. From the moment that he landed, stinking of cigarettes and already half drunk, I knew it was over. He opened the bottle of duty-free whiskey and became more belligerent when he realized I didn't want him there. My roommate, having grown up with an abusive stepfather, got scared and insisted that we leave our apartment.

I went to David's and she to her boyfriend's, leaving the ranting drunk in our apartment until he finally gave up and returned early to the UK. Being at David's felt safe and comfortable. He seemed so sane compared to the man who was sleeping in my bed. I told him, as he squeezed a blackhead on my shoulder, that Martin had said that I was the most beautiful person in the world. "You?" he said incredulously. We both cracked up, relieved at not being prey to that kind of romantic delusion.

From the beginning, David swore to not try to own me. I was free to sleep with whoever I wanted. I said that he was too. He didn't actually want to act on his own freedom, though. He was incapable of feeling desire towards another woman since he loved me. In a letter he wrote to me when I was in Cardiff, he said, "You don't know how happy it makes me to be able to drop my onerous burden with other women and just be yours."

In the margins, an arrow points to this line and in small print, he's added, "Ha! I don't mean your onerous burden. I mean yours, period."

The letter continues, "Lucky for the women, too, not to have to participate in my melodrama and I can be friendlier with them: a relief. I'm only in love with you and this is too obvious for everyone for anything else to be anything but ridiculous."

I also was obvious about my relationship with him. In fact, I often introduced him to a man that interested me. It was part of the seduction. I wanted the new man to see that I was involved with this beautiful being, involved in a way that was radical and unpossessive. David encouraged me. Sexually inexperienced, he would ask for details. Each one of my flings refreshed and enlivened our sex life. He admired my desire as much as he feared his inability to satisfy it.

When we got married six years later, we told ourselves that we were just doing it for our families. We were not buying into standard ideas of marriage, since we were keeping the relationship open. Full of anticipation and hope and desire, we were doing something as a man and a woman that felt like a commitment to a way of life. It united our intellectual practice with our belief systems. If we could see clearly the problems of possession and the fantasies of romantic love, our own love could survive.

Despite all our ideas about how different we were, our wedding was at the same church in Catalonia in which my parents and relatives had been married. I wore a big white dress and he wore a tux. I figured I was bucking the trend by insisting that both my parents walk me down the aisle, not just my father, who had expressed his disapproval of David. This just served to turn me against my dad even more, who I saw as a conservative who couldn't understand the bohemian lifestyle that we espoused. Plus, we were in my mother's land, so it was fitting that she be by my side as I walked towards David. I wasn't property that was going to be handed from one man to another.

The symbolism of both mother and father didn't really change much, of course. The marriage tradition is much heavier and monolithic than that.

One of the attendees was the pilot from Mallorca. David knew the story, so we made knowing and sarcastic comments about patriarchy and traffic in women. It was easier, as a twenty-five year old bride, to scorn convention than to feel brutalized by the rigid social relations around me. With my critical knowledge and my radical relationship, I felt superior to the aging pilot. He lived in a dishonest marriage. He was distinctly awkward around me. When he and his wife expressed their congratulations, I smiled at the man who had raped me, feeling that I had the upper hand. After all, I had a secret about him that could destroy his marriage. He had nothing on me, nothing my spouse didn't already know. Unlike that middle-aged couple, David and I would never be weighed down by tradition, gender roles, and expectations.

Armed with such assurance, we felt very confused when we went back to grad school as a married couple. Within days, we found ourselves playing house in our apartment. We set the table with our new wedding china and cooked ornate meals. We unconsciously recreated our family paradigms and emulated the parents whose mores we thought we resisted. We couldn't figure out how else to inhabit these new labels of "husband" and "wife."

Halfway through the meal I would yawn anxiously, trying to catch my breath. My stomach stabbed as I swallowed. Most times, I pushed my chair away from the table and lay on the floor. As soon as I did, I felt more comfortable, both physically and psychologically. My disruption of the conventional meal reasserted our difference from the norm of the bourgeois couple. With renewed appetite, David ate everything left on the table as I rested my calves across his lap and chatted to him from the floor.

Within months, I slept with someone else. It felt safer than ever to dally because we believed so strongly in our enduring relationship. The only restriction we placed on each other was that we weren't to fall in love with anyone else, which seemed like an easy one, since we were so much more intimate and honest with each other than anyone else could possibly be. We didn't yet see that those avowals were their own form of romantic illusion.

An open marriage didn't, in the end, work for us. Looking back on it, both separately and together, David and I think there are a few possible reasons:

- It was intellectually charming that, when we talked about our marriage, we said that it wasn't "to have and to hold" but to "halve and to hold." What we meant by it was that that we weren't trying to completely possess each other. Both of us saw how skittish I was at the thought of being trapped. Used to the clutching grip of Dolores's desire, I didn't imagine that you could "have" with an open palm, with fingers clasped enough to hold but loose enough to allow for movement. If I'd known it, I wonder if I could have demanded it of David.

As it was, he loved me intensely but diffusely, and I felt only half held by our relationship.
- He wasn't polyamorous, so he gave me all of himself. All his love and need and brilliance and anxiety and depression and mania and love. I felt responsible for him. He expected me to be able to hold him in all his contradictions. But in encouraging me to go elsewhere, he reaffirmed my belief that I was too much. No one wanted all of me. I was doing what I had learned as a child: to play the two mothers off each other, trying to get what I needed from first one, then the other. All my life, I had deflected admitting to myself that they were incapable of meeting my needs by bouncing back and forth between them. Now I was doing the same thing with men.
- We were so young and malleable that we shaped each other, cutting away the bits that we didn't like. When these ignored differences reemerged later in our marriage, they were devastating. We were so used to being in sync with each other, to being able to talk about anything, that our increased disagreements over work, money, child-rearing, and politics were unbearable rifts in the bedrock of our relationship.

Porous

I'd gotten drunk over the weekend, talking and talking to friends, spilling, indiscriminately pouring out affect. I had a vague memory of sitting in the back garden, smoking cigarettes with my neighbor, clutching her hand and kissing it as we told each other about our unhappy marriages.

Monday morning. Diarrhea. I had to stop at the McDonalds on my way to analysis because my insides were constricting, cramping, discharging.

I was disgusting.

Dr. O could not possibly want to know what I am, what I do. He could not possibly want me there.

Headache. It was like having a hard molded band around my skull. It hurt, this cast that held me hard while my insides — my guts and my brain — were turning to liquid and running out.

Dr. O said, "It's like you've never had the experience of being contained, of having something contain your overflow."

"You shouldn't bring that up. Don't offer it as a possibility because you can't be it. You can't be my container."

He said, "No."

And was silent as I cried.

That night I dreamt that my body was translucent, immaterial, and could easily be traversed by a school of fish that entered on one side and exited out the other. I was apprehensive when they approached, but their passing through me was nothing more than a soft pressure that made me queasy. They also experience queasiness, but there was something they liked about being able to traverse a body like that. They could penetrate so fully without resistance, without borders. Just a kind of tight hug, a feeling that they have never experienced before. They kept coming back for it. Addicted. Attracted. My body, in its absolute permeability, allowed them to go in wherever they wanted.

In Czesław Miłosz's poem, "Ars Poetica?" I read an image that evokes that porousness:

[…]
how difficult it is to remain just one person,
for our house is open, there are no keys in the doors,
and invisible guests come in and out at will.[24]

The self is many selves at once, crisscrossed through with other influences and visitors. It seemed so beautiful and true to me that it is "difficult […] to remain just one person," because, much as we want to lock those doors, they remain open. We want to believe that we are subject only to our own wills, and that we can be one hermetically sealed individual. In the dream, I am magical and open and giving. At the same time, I am penetrated at will. I can't keep my boundaries. I can't be wholly unto myself.

The next day, I said, "I'm relieved that you said 'No' about being my container."

I lay on the couch with that thought, checking to see if it was true. Was I really relieved? What if I was so in despair that I was devastated and just hunkered down? As the silent minutes passed, it became clearer to me. I did know. I didn't want him to try to be my guardian or my parent or a pair of arms that would hold me safe.

All my life I'd avoided exposure, seesawing between opening and shutting, exposing and hiding, feeling and numbing, knowing and ignoring. I had an acute sense of when something crossed my personal limits, or when I crossed someone else's. I would feel that incursion to be "too much," something that threatened the containment that I needed to feel. I didn't believe that I could be in my own skin and allow it to be a porous membrane that would let things in and out.

It was not only intrusive others that were "too much." I was as well. As a child at the *finca*, I was, for my mother, too fat, too tomboyish, too American, too Central American in my accent. The rest of the year in the States, I was too ambitious, too flirtatious, too emotional, too needy, too attention-seeking, too talkative. My desires and enthusiasms always seemed to overflow the tight confines that I was supposed to fit into. Those confines were invisible but felt. Sometimes they held me safe. Other times they kept me captive in their tight constraint. Often they were a vessel too small to contain my outpouring.

I said, "I don't even have an image for what a container for myself would be." I considered different images — a box, an egg, a bag. None captured that mix of too muchness and tight constraint that I was struggling with.

All of a sudden, it came to me. "There was this toy we had when I was a kid. It was made of metal overlapping petals that spin open to reveal a hidden secret when you press the base. Then the spinning slows down and it closes tight like a band. The opening part is so joyous, all exuberant and alive in the way that the petals fling themselves back and open. When it closes, it's tight and protected. Nothing can be seen of what is inside it. That's my image. Open, shut. Open, shut."

Its Own World

Cada matrimonio es un mundo. Every marriage is a world. This refrain is one that I often heard on the lips of my mother and her sisters when they sat around the tea table at the *finca*. It was usually accompanied with a shrug at the end of a gossip session about a couple, to imply that there must be other unseen binding aspects of the dysfunctional relationship they had just dissected.

In the first few years that David and I were together, I think we probably seemed, at least to our peers if not to my father, like a well-suited couple. We were both doing PhDs (he was at Princeton, but because of the big grant he'd received, could afford to spend semesters at Duke with me), so we shared our writing and our ideas. We took long walks with our lanky yellow dog, read books, and hung out a lot with friends. A few times, we were asked if we were siblings, both curly-haired and tall, full of a vitality and energy that came from our long hours of sleep, copious exercise, and healthy eating. We were obviously best friends, so closely intertwined that it was rare for us to be in the same space without winding our limbs around each other. We decided to have a baby not so much because we wanted a child but because it seemed like the ultimate expression of our deep and unshakeable love for each other. The emergence of our beautiful boys from my body was a wondrous manifestation of the capacity of our love to create someone new.

Yet we also fought a lot. There were times I stormed out of the apartment, or off the bus, or into the woods, certain I never wanted to see him again. We argued about external things, like whether the person who had cut him off in traffic was right or wrong, or whether voting was democratic or a means to maintain the status quo. Our emotions ramped up quickly, and within minutes my face would be red with rage. One time I threw a stick at him. Another time I hit his back with my fists. These tantrum-like rages were so out of character from my more common tactics of icy verbal violence that they startled us. Scared, we would start to laugh. That laughter proved to us that we were okay with each other. Our conflicts were just expressions of the brutal honesty that defined our relationship. Volatility felt like security. It was more reliable than the romantic protestations of constancy that more ordinary couples around us made.

As the years wore on, however, it was no longer charming. He antagonized colleagues and administration at every academic job he got. In part, it was because he was committed to spending time with Sebastian, so he would miss department meetings or arrive late because he'd been climbing the monkey bars at the playground. It was also because he was hot-headed, and a man that tall and loud could be very scary when he got mad. The third-year review for the tenure-track position that he held at a small liberal arts college in Pennsylvania came back with praise for his research but with some serious red flags about his behavior. I was pregnant with Liam, and nervous that he would not get tenure. So, in 1999, when I got a good job offer in the mid-West, we decided that he should quit and use the time to write the book on Puritans for which he had just received a prestigious National Endowment for the Humanities fellowship.

When his father found out that David had left his position to follow me, he said, "Your wife won't respect you if you don't have a job." We marveled at how sexist he was. Childcare and writing *were* real jobs. Equally thankless jobs, we soon realized. Neither of us were cut out for full-time childcare. Too ambitious and impatient, we would get bored and crabby spending twenty-four hours with the boys that we adored. Within weeks of our move to Illinois, we realized that David wasn't getting anything done on his book, so we hired nannies and babysitters to give him time.

A decade later, there was still no book. In that time, he hadn't had a job or brought in anything more than the stipend for an occasional sessional class. We had followed my career to Argentina, England, and Toronto. I had tenure, but my generous salary couldn't cover the growing debt that accrued with every year of his unemployment.

His brilliance began to manifest less as fascinating conversations and more as erratic routines. The children were always late for school and without their lunches. Our household was chaotically disorganized. The only way I could handle it was to have massive cleaning purges every month or so, when I would throw too many things out, incapable of establishing order. It still makes me sad, to think about the keepsakes that I jettisoned in my desperation to get rid of clutter.

It seemed impossible to have the kind of household that I had grown up in, or the one that my sister, a stay-at-home mother, had. But somehow, despite the fact that I came home from work to make dinner every night, I didn't cut myself some slack and understand that I was the breadwinner and that David was far from a domestic homemaker. I still expected us to have an orderly life. We certainly weren't living the oppressively bourgeois life of our parents, but the failures to live it carried their own weight.

The few times we fought in front of Sebastian and Liam made us feel ashamed and immature. To scare the boys with our uncontrollable anger wasn't honest, it was irresponsible and selfish. We were consumed with care and anxiety and bitter anger.

Finally, when the boys were eleven and seven, I left him, certain that our marriage was over. I had never lived on my own before, and didn't really know what to do with myself when I didn't have the kids. I dated a man who was intellectual and insightful, but who expected a level of presence and commitment that I couldn't give. The pressure made me anxious, and I tried to hide from him how divided I truly was. When we were together, I missed my children. And I missed how David had put so few demands on me, never expecting me to be more than half there.

After a few months, I broke up with the man, and David and I got back together. All it involved was moving back into the house that he had refused to leave when we separated. It seemed like some of the things that bothered me had changed. He had taken cooking classes and begun to make elaborate meals for the boys. He said that he understood the stress I had been under for so long. We figured things had changed. I was reassured by the ease with which we still laughed together, and moved by the familiar comfort of tender love.

We both wanted things to be different. We decided to close the marriage and swear monogamy to each other. The promises and charts and schedules that we made to organize our lives quickly fell apart as we got caught up in the old patterns of my demanding impatience and his passive-aggressive resistance. Looking back, I see how much earnestness and fear went into these efforts. We knew we didn't work well together, but we were so attached and so in love. It seemed impossible to split us apart.

Too Much

Whenever someone asked me how my analysis was going, I never knew what to say. I didn't feel like anything was happening. I wasn't having huge realizations, or making concerted decisions. I knew *how* it was going — crying, shuddering, freaking out, long silences — but I didn't know *what* it was doing or if I was learning anything.

What I didn't realize was how much my intellectual work was changing. The project on sound in Latin America was going nowhere. I didn't want to tether myself to a particular topic and set of texts, the way I had pre-tenure. To focus on national literatures felt like an arbitrary demarcation that is not in keeping with how texts are actually produced, which is obviously in dialogue with other countries, traditions, influences, and issues. I wanted to teach ideas, not places. Now, with tenure, I didn't have to continue doing Latin American Studies. I could organize my courses and my research around a different set of concerns.

Without thinking about it too much, I began to teach very long novels slowly. Starting with some of the big fat books that I had read as a child, and again for my comprehensive exams at Duke, I assigned George Eliot and Charles Dickens in my course "Affinities: Readings in Realism and Radicalism." I allowed half the course for each writer, justifying my extended mode of teaching as historically accurate, since these novels were originally published serially and read in weekly installments. "Don't read ahead," I would say to my students. "Instead, let's spend time attending to not only the content, but also the style, cadence, and syntax."

The Victorian novels that I was teaching were full of twists and coincidences. Though I loved reading them as much as I always had, I was a little frustrated by all the "ah-ha" moments and the neat tying up of disparate threads. It felt, especially after all the incoherence I was encountering with Dr. O, artificial.

So the urge grew in me, to continue to teach long novels, but to explore how the form changed in the beginning of the twentieth century, with the advent of cinema and psychoanalysis. My problem was that I had managed to conduct my whole literary career without ever having read anything in the field of Modernism. I decided to turn this to my advantage, teaching classes in which I, alongside my students, encountered for the first time James Joyce's *Ulysses*, Thomas Mann's *The Magic Mountain*, and Marcel Proust's *In Search of Lost Time*. To justify this unorthodox way of teaching, I called upon Jacques Rancière's argument for a democratic mode of teaching. His "ignorant schoolmaster" does not teach from a position of knowledge, in which the student is seen as ignorant. Rather, he teaches from his own position of ignorance.[25] I had learned enough, in my analysis, to sense that "not knowing" could be a productive place from which to think, and I wanted to encounter the texts alongside my students.

These books excited me, felt so huge and true. They also exhausted me, and I recoiled from the time and energy that they required. They were big, excessive, self-absorbed, boring, long-winded, time-consuming—too much! Proust, for instance, seemed so self-indulgent, with his long sentences and excursus. A student showed me photos of Proust's *paperoles*, the cut-out scraps of paper that he pasted to his manuscript pages in order to add edits, addenda, and afterthoughts, much to his publisher's dismay. They were a very literal visual depiction of the incapacity of the standard form of the novel to contain his words.

Before class, dread would lie heavy in my gut, mimicking the feeling I often had before analysis. I didn't know anything, I had no idea what to say, I couldn't possibly lead a seminar on a book as hard as *Ulysses*. Despite proclaiming myself to be the ignorant schoolmaster, Joyce made me feel *too* ignorant. I even tried to quit, suggesting to my students that we could just stop reading it, that there was no requirement that said we had to finish it. They refused to leave it halfway, so we blundered through together. I'm so glad we did. It was worth it all for Molly Bloom's "and yes I said yes I will Yes" that ends the book.

As my students and I read these long novels slowly, we encountered our own boredom and disappointment. Sometimes these books had ideas that were not fleshed out, other times the loose ends were not tied up. We had to resist our usual academic attempts at mastery, holding off on our interpretations. Reading this way allowed us to hear the nuances and meanings that permeated the writing, and taught us to listen to moments in the books that may have passed unperceived in our more usual mode of consumption. I hadn't set out to teach the Lacanian injunction of "Don't try to understand," but that was what we were doing, paying attention to seemingly insignificant details or contradictions in a process that was very similar to what Dr. O and I did, day after day.

Into the Destructive Element

David and I went, in early spring, to the beach with the boys and one of their friends. As we often did when on an outing, we fought. It was stressful changing subway and streetcars with distracted boys and hyper dog. He took it out on a driver who honked at us when we didn't clear the crosswalk in time. I pulled the boys away, all of us embarrassed by his public display of anger. When he caught up to us on the cold windswept sand, he and I argued, me bitterly rational, him emotionally distraught. All of a sudden, he just walked away from me, towards the water. He didn't stop as the frigid waves started lapping at his feet, knees, hips, down jacket. The boys and I yelled for him to come back, worried for him and ashamed that an outsider, their friend, was witnessing so much of David's volatile behavior. When I heard the tremor of fear in Sebastian's voice as he called out to his father, fury washed over me.

When he was only eleven, Sebastian had said, as I picked stuff up off the floor, that it was really like I had three children, not two. I felt vindicated — even my kid could see how messed up our family was — but also horrified that a boy should live with parents like us. He needed a father figure. Instead, he was so much more responsible than David that I relied on him as if he was my partner, and hated myself and David for it.

We got back from the beach and Sebastian ran up to his room and slammed his door. I went up and listened to him describe his humiliation through angry tears. The next day I couldn't stop my own crying rage. Dr. O talked more than he ever had, saying things like, "So there's an order to who listens to whom in your family?" and "What are the things you all hear that aren't said?" and "Ah, what you resist hearing." I liked that he was talking, but I didn't understand his cryptic words. They just made me cry harder, and I felt panicky that I had let David's overwhelming presence into the room. I had allowed Dr. O to hear about the craziness of my husband. And it made him talk.

The next day I called Dr. O to task. "Your comments about my family dynamic were sympathetic. You acted as my ally against my husband. That was what Wendy would do when I would tell her a story about how crazy David was. Or what a girlfriend would do. But you, you're not supposed to just take my side. Instead, I want you to disrupt the coherent story that I told you, in which I was the wronged wife and mother. The only way I can prevent it from happening again is if you resist it somehow."

Dr. O said, "What if the story yesterday is about you? About how you want to keep everything under a control and yet you want to go out into the dark deep waters?"

"That would mean that I put David in the crazy role so that I don't have to think about the ways that I am losing it."

I paused for a long time, and then continued, "You know, you have no idea what my life is like outside the space of this room. You don't know what my fights with David are like. Or how I flip out at the kids. You also don't see how competent I am at work, giving pieces of myself away, trying hard to make them good pieces — of intellect and beauty and authority and sexiness — even though I'm so exhausted and drained that I can barely do it."

He said, "The sealskin."

I said, "There is no center. All the pieces are flying off."

He said, "No parental authority to hold them."

Not Knowing

I trudged across the light dusting of snow, my head bent down towards the sidewalk. I was thinking of nothing in particular when I startled myself by saying, quite clearly and with a shrug of my shoulders, "I don't know." Oh great, now I was talking to myself? I kept my mouth shut as I turned onto his sidewalk, but I heard the repeated words, keeping tempo with my steps: I don't know. I don't know. I don't know. I walked past his house, and looked up, confused about where I was. As I backtracked, I shook my head in disbelief at myself, once again muttering out loud, "I don't know."

The tone in my voice was strangely wry. It had a kind of old man comic intonation, as if I were both world-weary and off-handed. To an outsider, it may have sounded like I was accepting my not knowing, but I was panicky. Dr. O's questions or even his slightest "hmmm" never let me ignore how little I knew about what I thought, felt, or was going to say.

My recurring dreams of the ocean seemed to signal my fear of standing on the brink of a terrifying immersion into all the things that I didn't know. I didn't want to plunge in, the way David had. I began blanking out on the couch. Losing my train of thought. Not remembering what I was saying, what he had said. Crying and then just stopping, unsure of what I was even crying about. It was a familiar feeling: a thick blanket of fog, a wall that I hit up against. I had told him early on that it was one of the reasons that I wanted to do psychoanalysis, that I felt intellectually hemmed in by an inability to take a thought as far as I should. I'd forgotten that reason as I lay on the couch free-associating about sex, childhood memories, stories, and books. But now it was back, the inability to stay with a thought, to persevere in the difficult challenge.

I found it almost impossible to reside, as Dr. O seemed to, in a space of not knowing as we hit up against my resistances. Unlike Wendy or other conventional weekly therapists, Dr. O held off on interpretation. I read a line in Allison Bechdel's *Are You My Mother?* that helped me understand this. She quotes Winnicott saying:

> It appalls me to think how much deep change I have prevented or delayed in patients [...] by my personal need to interpret. If only we can wait, the patient arrives at understanding creatively and with immense joy, and I now enjoy this joy more than I used to enjoy the sense of having been clever.[26]

A psychoanalyst, it seems, learns that the structural delay of knowledge brings a different kind of insight. Timing is everything. The recognition of a contradiction and its underlying conflict has to come from the analysand herself. If it comes, instead, from the analyst, it doesn't get transformed into knowledge and practice.

This seemed exactly what Dr. O and I were doing. My resistance was keeping me in a state of ignorance as long as necessary, until the truth revealed itself with such insistence that I could recognize and internalize it.

I begged him at the end of a session to not send me away without waking me up first. He said, "Hypnosis...."

Cockroaches

David and I used to go to a remote island in Georgian Bay where his parents had a dilapidated cottage. With no running water or electricity, we cleared paths through the hoarded detritus of his eccentric parents, and tried to stay outside as much as possible. The daytime was stunning. Blue sky and water, pink sinuous rocks, clumps of tiger lilies and wild blueberries. We canoed out to windswept islands and toasted sandwiches over an open fire. I told David that I wanted my ashes scattered in that wild and desolate landscape.

The nights, though, were the gruesome counterpoint to all that beauty. The uninsulated wood frame shack creaked and groaned. The mosquitoes feasted on us. The kerosene light sputtered and smelled. We had to pump water to do dishes in the dark stained sink, and boil water to drink. I'd say that I couldn't stand it up there anymore, that I wanted to leave and never come back.

When Sebastian was a baby, we spent the entire month of June up there. Our yellow dog slept on clumps of dry yellow grass, curled up like the snakes that we sometimes saw. The Northern Lights danced in the sky in the chilly evenings. One night, I was sitting in front of the fireplace nursing Sebastian to sleep in the rocking chair. I heard a scuttling sound, and looked up to see cockroaches swarming down the wood slats of the walls, drawn out by the heat of the fire. I almost screamed but didn't want to startle my drowsy sucking son, blissfully unaware of my racing heart and crawling skin. I calmed my breathing as I held my bare feet a couple of inches above the ground, trying to have no contact with the house around me.

David reassured me by telling me that his parents just called them pine bugs. Maybe a rose by another name wouldn't smell so sweet, but a large glistening brown bug with wiry legs and long antennae was going to freak me out no matter what it was called.

In those first years, we talked about improvements that could be done to the place. Solar panels, a water pump, repairs, cleaning, and a reliable fridge would have done wonders. But he dreamt of even more, and talked about skylights and lofts and cubbies and window seats and investors and retreats. Each summer, however, was not the time to begin on any of the ideas. He was occupied with writing a book or helping his elderly mother clamber over the rocks to the outhouse. Instead of doing the renovations, we spent most of the time we were there talking about them. I got tired of all the plans, the glass castles that took up so much of our imagination and energy. We took to calling the place "the shit shack" and sleeping in a tent on the porch so as to avoid the spiders, mosquitoes, and roaches.

Every time we'd pack to drive up there from Toronto, it would take us hours to get out of the house. I'd wake up early and cook for the week, so as to not have to use the kitchen up there. Once I had the food stored in containers and the bags ready to go, David would somehow complicate things, not remembering how to mount the canoe on top of the car, or repacking the trunk with safety precautions in mind. We'd usually get into a huge fight, the kids scurrying back into the house to play video games and avoid being near us.

It would be late afternoon by the time we spilled out of the car and dragged down the narrow dock the duffel bags, coolers, toys, book bags, dog food, sleeping bags, Legos, and groceries procured along the way.

David didn't believe in polluting the lake, so he refused to use his parents' old motor boat to get to the island, seven miles from the mainland. Instead, we loaded up the canoe with all that stuff, plus two boys, a dog, and a cat, and he and I paddled out.

Once, we let the cat out of her carrier because we couldn't stand her howling anymore. We figured she would enjoy her freedom and just prowl the bottom of the canoe. Instead, she caught a glimpse of a nearby rocky coast, and dove into the water, swimming like an otter to get to shore. The canoe almost capsized as David lurched to grab her by the tail and deposit the sodden limp mass of miserable creature into the boat.

For the next three hours of paddling, she mewed piteously, the boys bickered, the dog whined. David talked over it all, fresh on a rant about big corporations, decreasing water levels, and the greedy stupidity of other cottage owners.

It got dark. When the island finally loomed before us over the water, I leaned over the edge and navigated our way between the shoals with the sputtering light of an old flashlight. We released the cat, who ran off into the bushes and didn't emerge again for two days. Silently, I hauled our suitcases and crawled into bed, trying not to shine the lantern on the walls of the cottage. I was scared of what I would see.

The One

Analysis was becoming more and more opaque. I had a creeping sense that I needed to address the problems in my marriage. I wasn't. I felt like I was postponing everything, waiting for things to happen instead of making them happen. Waiting for the analysis to do whatever it was supposed to do. Waiting for something to come clear about my family, about my work, about myself.

"Waiting is so passive!" I said to Dr. O. "It's intolerable. I want action. I want to feel like the agent of my life."

The metaphor I blurted out next proved, however, that I was still waiting for something to be done to me instead of me doing. "I want to be fucked up the ass. And have it matter." Immediately, I was embarrassed to be so crude, to say something that seemed to come from nowhere.

Dr. O said, "You want a magical solution? A transformation that will release something? Allow you to get your head out of your ass?"

"I want to be able to *know*."

My head, though, felt very far up the convoluted recesses of something I didn't know. Whatever it was, I feared knowing it despite my protestations. I didn't understand anything. I felt furious at Dr. O, and increasingly desperate to escape the darkness that seemed to engulf us the second I started talking.

Could I have done something else than what I did next? Could I have been braver and just stayed in there with the somber truths that were emerging about my psyche?

I don't know because I didn't.

Instead, I "acted out." Acting out, in psychoanalysis, refers to the actions that the analysand takes outside of the sessions. In a displaced way, these actions manifest something that she has not been able to express in the analysis. In the sessions, I was hitting up against something that was repressed in my unconscious. I couldn't remember it but I could do it. To do it was to act out the deep spiraling structures of seduction, splitting, hiding, and destroying that shaped my past and informed my present.

In retrospect, it seems inevitable that I started to have an affair with a married man. We'd been acquainted for years, and we had met each others' spouses and children. When we saw each other at university meetings, he had the tendency to turn innocuous comments into innuendos. He touched my arm when we talked, and stood a little too close. I always kept my distance.

It wasn't till the day when I saw him act decisively in a leadership role at an important meeting that I reciprocated his flirtation. Like a repetition of the skating scene with David, I was swept off my feet by this man's power, and excited that he was attracted to me. We went out to celebrate his speech with other people. And then we stayed out after everyone else went home. Alcohol lubricated that first evening (and many of the other ones). He and I groped each other in an alley. As I pressed against him and felt his desire, words came tumbling out of me, the opposite of the long blank silences of analysis. I warned him, in the sexiest way I could, that he should know what he was getting into because I was demanding. I was excessive. I was hungry. I elicited promises and wove fantasies. The ugly duckling whose head was submerged in the murk of analysis all of a sudden was transformed into a powerful swan.

Hungover and shaky the next day, I told Dr. O how I had felt an exhilarating loss of self. Then I heard myself say something that I didn't know was in my head: *Maybe he's the one.* It startled me.

"That's weird," I said. "I don't think I even believe in 'the one.' And I didn't think I was looking for him! I am married, after all. Despite the trouble, David is my love."

A part of me didn't want to get involved in something that would consume so much of my energy and attention. But another part was dying to have something into which to escape, head to tail. I did write the man an email, attempting to stop it before it started. I wrote that I really wanted to be with him and that it broke my heart to say no. But that my heart was already broken — by my husband who I loved but who had failed my trust, by my parents who gave me away. I told him that yes, his hunch was right — men did fall in love with me, but that was because I needed them to, and I couldn't love them back because nothing could fix the brokenness.

After I sent it to him, I forwarded it to my friend Catherine. She said it was a ridiculously provocative break-up letter, a "come hither" disguised as a sad and genuine farewell. One that I had engineered so as to necessitate a face-to-face conversation. To which I wore, without admitting it to myself, sexy underwear. And to which I brought the keys to a friend's empty apartment, which was around the corner from the cafe that I chose for our meeting. Within an hour, we were on her bed, undressing each other with ravenous desire.

Cuckoo

It was Christmas time and Dr. O was taking two weeks off. He was leaving even though I was trying to be a good analysand, free associating and making interesting connections. Okay, well, I was having an affair, but other than that I was trying hard!

"How could you send me away?" I sobbed.

We had talked about ducks and swans in analysis, but now a Magnetic Fields tune popped into my head that brought another bird to our discussion:

> Don't fall in love with me yet
> We only recently met
> [...] It's only fair to tell you I'm absolutely cuckoo.[27]

I was cuckoo. Cuckoo to carry on an affair while maintaining the roles of professor, mother, wife, and analysand. Cuckoo to have frequent trysts and to feel so much love and lust and longing. But that's what cuckoos are like: big birds who demand too much. Cuckoos lay their eggs in another species' nest. The foster parents raise the cuckoo as one of their chicks, despite its inexhaustible hunger. An intruder, a parasite, a burden; its name becomes synonymous with craziness. What is it that makes the cuckoo crazy? To have been born into a foreign nest, to be bigger than the other chicks, to demand that its basic needs be met by adults who are not its parents.

My feeling that Dr. O was rejecting me and abandoning me was so raw that I was ashamed. I felt skinless. I wished for thick blankets to cover myself, since there were not enough clothes that I could put on to protect myself from this exposure. I was shaking uncontrollably.

He was silent. I wouldn't have been able to hear him even if he had said anything, since I was hyperventilating so much.

Abruptly I went completely still and began to breathe quietly. My mind was empty as I floated at a calm distance from the crazy excess of emotion that I had just displayed.

"I'm done. You're not going to respond, you're just going to go ahead and go away. I'm not going to humiliate myself in front of you."

He said, "And that's our time for today." I swung my feet down to the ground and walked purposely out the door.

After New Year's, I went back, and the instant I lay on the couch I began shaking again, the exact same feeling of naked exposure washing over me. Right back where I had left off.

Leda and the Swan

My bon-vivant uncle visited Toronto from Spain. We went out to lunch with my lover, who posed as a colleague and nothing more. My uncle, apropos of nothing, pointed to me and said, "This is the woman about whom her father says that she can't get in a taxi without the driver wanting to take her to dinner." I didn't understand why he said it, and to whom. It was as if he was winking at my lover, trying to excite his interest in me. Or to say to me, "We all know what you do to men."

It was such an uncanny thing to hear. My father had spoken to another man about how I wielded a certain power. But is it power if you don't know you have it? Or if you can't really manage it? If I was so powerful, why had I often felt so helpless when I was hit on?

The man that made me feel most helpless was my father himself. I wondered if I still would have been as desperate for sex and power and the male gaze as an adult if I had been able to get his attention when I was a girl. I feared that my way of being in the world could be summed up with the devastating phrase "daddy issues."

When I recounted the incident to Dr. O, he said, "So basically, your uncle said, 'Here's Leda.'"

This was in reference to a poem I had brought up before: W.B. Yeats's "Leda and the Swan." Even though I hadn't read it since undergrad poetry class, I often remembered the image of a sexual union between a muscly feathered creature and soft human flesh, and the way that once the sexual act is completed, the body is "dropped with indifferent beak." That phrase seemed to capture what I was experiencing in the affair: pendulum swings from the flurry of passion to a cold and angry disinterest.

But wait, who did what in the poem? Of course, it was Leda who was raped by Zeus the swan who drops her with "indifferent beak." So why had I conflated the aggressor and the victim in my head? I seemed to inhabit all the subject positions in the poem, knowing, viscerally, the swan's lust and ensuing apathy, and at the same time Leda's astonished yet erotic fear of being the desired object of such a powerful creature.

I went home and reread the poem and found that my confusion was not unfounded. It's not just that he takes something from her by assaulting her sexually. The poem ends with the suggestion that she takes something as well:

> Did she put on his knowledge with his power
> Before the indifferent beak could let her drop?[28]

This felt logical to me. Unwanted sexual encounters with older men had sometimes been the price I had paid for what felt like an access to knowledge and power. How many men had spoken to me, the young, eager, interested woman in front of them, in slightly patronizing tones about their expertise? And how had they changed their attitude to me as they began to desire me more? In bed with me, they saw me as wondrous. Empowered by their admiration, I could talk knowledgeably and engagingly, eliciting their intellectual as well as their sexual attention.

When I was an undergraduate and first read the poem, I also read Camille Paglia's *Sexual Personae*. I remember disagreeing with her interpretation of the line, "a shudder in the loins." She says that it is "both the rapist's climax and the victim's fright."[29] Why couldn't the shudder be the victim's climax and the rapist's fright? It seemed to me that Zeus had more taken from him than Leda did.

So the next day I came in and said all this to Dr. O. About how I had a pattern in which I seduced men to profit from their power, gain their knowledge, and then discard them. I felt brave and defiant to admit such despicable behavior, to show him the disdain I had for notions of sexual inviolability. I had figured out a way to disinvest these violations of their power by seeing sex as a source of self-empowerment. I could eroticize the awkward, uneven, dangerous, or harmful encounters with men, and believe myself to be an astute and savvy woman who chose to get something out of the situation.

"If I'm Leda, it's because I take knowledge and power. I use my sexual power to my advantage. I need you to know that I am not a passive victim. I'm active in these encounters. If they are acts of misconduct, I am guilty."

I still admire his response, because I know that if a young woman said that to me, I would accept it, afraid that if I didn't I would be labelling her as a victim. Dr. O didn't see my declaration as definitive. He said, "Sexuality can act like a hardening, a scabbing over of a wound."

This hit me hard, because I didn't want to see myself as wounded, as acting out of pain. Everything I had learned as a feminist was about my sexual empowerment and agency. But I was also tired of the defiant stance that I had just performed for him. I didn't want to be an angry seductress who dropped men with indifferent beak once I had profited from their power and gained their knowledge.

It seemed to me that I was asking the wrong questions. Instead of "who was taking" and "what was being taken" in every sexual encounter, I could, in the calm and nonjudgmental space of the analysis, ask, "What am I so angry about? What am I so turned on by? What always hurts that I am trying to numb through sex?"

Dr. O was suggesting that I used seduction as a coping strategy. This made me describe a recent rape dream in which once again I tried to sweet-talk the man out of the torture he was inflicting on me. When the violence became too intense, I went limp and quiet. Dr. O asked if this was a game rule for me. In the face of bullies and extortion and brutality and violence, did I go deep into the pain so as to numb it? Or did I just go blank?

I said, "When you stand in cold water, it hurts so much that you want to just run back onto the sand. But you can override your impulse to leave and go in deeper until your body is numb." I refused, at that moment and for years afterwards, to think of David, standing in the waves, trying to escape the bully that was me, the violence that had become our marriage. And to know that both of us were trying to numb our pain.

Animation

When I had walked into analysis after that first impetuous afternoon in my friend's apartment, Dr. O said, deadpan, "Selkie has found her skin?"

It did feel good to be in my skin as it was stroked. It was a return to the immersive element, the sea of sex in which I happily swam. So I didn't let myself think about what his statement implied: that I had found my slick skin in the caress of a man, slipping away once again into the murky ocean. It's like I still saw Dr. O as the captor who wanted to keep me on dry land.

"The analysis is too stringent," I said. "Why not take the open arms, the unwarranted in-love-ness of a man? Even if I know now that it's not what I really want, that what I've always already wanted is my parents' love. I'm obviously too much, gotta take my excess elsewhere. Always have been: too much for my parents, who paid someone to cuddle and clean and feed and nurture me; too much for Dolores, who couldn't talk to me about books or come to school events or pay for my education and activities; too much for my siblings, who teased me for my Spanish; too much for my Spanish relatives, who criticized my American body and habits."

I usually managed this feeling of too muchness by performing a self-assured calm with everyone around me. I distributed it amongst them, carefully accounting for how much I gave to each so as to balance it. I was an easy daughter, never arguing or protesting. I maintained a smooth exterior that repelled my parents' or Dolores's questions or concern. No one knew how much I partitioned off, either through the masturbatory fantasy life that acted like a thick padding around me, or through the lies and deceit that allowed me to escape into wild flings and dangerous situations.

To escape from a troubled marriage to the eager body of a lover, and then to bounce back to the familiarity of domesticity and intimacy when I was exhausted by the sex and secrecy: this was an oscillation and rhythm that made me feel alive. I had something so excessive and vibrant that I couldn't show it to just one person.

As I wrote fictional meetings into my calendar, claiming important work dinners and drinks with colleagues, I was balancing this split. I reserved cheap hotels in parts of the city that neither I nor the man ever frequented. We met, postponing deadlines and skimping on class prep or committee work. Gleeful the second we closed the door, we entered into the intense state of physicality that we both craved. The risk was worth it. We were animated by each other, capable of action and energy and decision and drive.

After we checked out a few hours later, we'd go drink beer and make out in dive bars. As we got tipsy, we talked about our kids, or bemoan how unsatisfying our sweet spouses were. We insisted that we were committed to our marriages, and couldn't imagine disrupting the families that we had. We liked to imagine what it would be like to be a couple, though it was never quite convincingly fleshed out in details. What neither of us could admit was that we were so fundamentally different in terms of our interests and predilections that if it had not been for the sex, we would never have gotten together in the first place.

I was exhausted. He and I coped with our guilt by hypnotizing ourselves, fucking so as to fall into a reverie in which we each believed that we weren't hurting our loved ones. Everything was hallucinatorily vivid, colored by the intensity. That color was a welcome antidote to the perpetual grey fog of analysis, to the monotony of my daily life of work and chaotic home life.

When I went home, I read books to my children and tidied up the house and walked the dog and stayed up writing my lover erotic messages so that David would be asleep by the time I lay down next to him. I slept only to wake up a couple of hours later, my gut churning with guilt and fear. What was I doing? How could I continue to do something so harmful and deceitful and selfish?

I had to end it. In an email that was similar to the initial attempt at stopping it before it started, I wrote to the man after a particularly glorious day together, telling him that it was too disruptive and divisive, and that I needed to end it. We wouldn't be going to the hotel I had reserved for later in the week. The emails between us for the next twenty-four hours went from sad to angry to panicked to verbosely serious, and back again.

Finally, we agreed to meet in person to stop writing. Guess where we chose to talk about how we were never going to sleep together again? At the diner across the street from the hotel that still held my uncancellable reservation. Guess when? At noon: check-in time. The second we saw each other's faces we both started crying. The waitress brought us coffee as we sobbed. I tried to explain myself but the words were unconvincing, and our tears were speaking so much more eloquently than any of the reasoned arguments I had prepared. Within minutes we left some money on the table and checked into our room.

The second we were in the room together we clasped each other, terrified that we had ever thought to give it all up. Even though it was making our ordinary lives untenable, we couldn't forfeit it, couldn't possibly imagine living without the high it gave us.

The next day, Dr. O said that I was immersing myself in the bodily elements. That I couldn't decide to do analysis because then I'd have to stop doing, and if I stopped doing, I'd be trapped.

I couldn't imagine what "not doing" would look like. I didn't even understand what he meant. I had already decided to do analysis. I was, I thought, already doing it.

Error

"I may have erred about the Proust."

Dr. O was referring to our session two days earlier, when I had talked about Dolores going back to El Salvador for a month when I was ten. Before she left for the airport, she had kissed me repeatedly, crying that she didn't want to leave me alone for so long. That night, I lay on top of my bed clutching my oversized stuffed polar bear and sobbing. Loudly. I wanted my mother to hear my lonely despair, though I was simultaneously embarrassed by my excessive emotion. As I wailed, part of me wondered if I was acting, if I was really that sad. What was I trying to achieve with that loudness?

Telling Dr. O, I began to cry, caught up in the conundrum of wanting to be acknowledged while fearing judgment. In a repetition of my childhood suspicion, I distrusted my tears. I wondered, from a distance that made it seem as if I were hovering above myself, if my crying was an attention-seeking ploy used to elicit belief and pity.

This all made me think of the early scene in Marcel Proust's *In Search of Lost Time,* in which Marcel lies in bed wishing for his mother's goodnight kiss. He gets increasingly anxious and overwrought, so much so that his parents take pity on him and his mother sleeps in his room that night. It is both a victory and defeat, since he got the thing he most wanted at the expense of his mother seeing him as weak and fragile. It is not until he is older that he can begin to understand how fundamental that contradiction has been in his life. In the isolation of his quiet cork-lined room, he puts into words those inchoate feelings that until now have hovered in his unconscious:

> But of late I have been increasingly able to catch, if I listen attentively, the sound of the sobs [...]. In reality their echo has never ceased; it is only because life is now growing more and more quiet round about me that I hear them anew, like those convent bells which are so effectively drowned during the day by the noises of the street that one would suppose them to have been stopped, until they sound out again through the silent evening air.[30]

I wasn't crying as I described this scene in detail, but I was still very caught up in the poignancy of the sobs that have always been there, and that I was beginning to hear in myself through the "attentive listening" of analysis.

Interrupting my train of thought, Dr. O said, "Abstracting strong emotion through a turn to literature?"

I went silent. And then, forcefully, I said, "You know that's not true! That moment in Proust breaks me open. It allows me to hear and access something in myself that is closer than I could get if I just described it in myself. You should already know that about me, that talking about books is not a way to get distance, but rather to feel more and to bring those feelings into language."

The next day, I lay on the couch for a long time. I didn't know why I was silent; I just knew that I didn't want to talk. When I finally did, I talked about the craziness of my life. I was hosting a guest speaker, Liam had gotten in trouble at school, David was depressed but had taken up juggling, my lover and I had just had a late-night tryst, and I had to write a piece for my critical writing class on Barthes's *A Lover's Discourse*. It wasn't only my husband who was juggling balls aloft. Dr. O said little.

The next day, as soon as I lay down, he said, "I may have erred about the Proust."

An error. He had strayed from the right path, imposing an interpretation that may have been true for others, but not for me. And I had known it. Unlike other times, when I may have ceded to his presumed authority, this time I had insisted on my own truth. I had never before thought that Dr. O imposed some external interpretive tenet, but his immediate interpretation — literature equals abstraction — seemed like something he had learned in his training, like he had responded in a knee-jerk way instead of actually listening to how meaningful that Proust passage was to me. In doing so, he himself had deflected the pain of what I was saying by accusing me of deflecting it. The fact that he admitted it to me was vital to keeping my trust.

As the relief washed over me that he believed me, I asked him, with tears in my eyes, "Do you think I'm manic?"

He paused, then responded, "I think you're in a lot of pain and you don't know if there's any other way to deal with it than to keep jumping."

This was a more compassionate response than what I had expected, which was for him to remain silent, or to say that I do instead of think. This time, however, he responded to the sobs as a manifestation of an emotion, not as a hysterical demand for attention. This acknowledgment allowed me to recognize them as real. He and I were beginning to hear the sobs that had always already been there, unheard, unspoken, unknown.

L'inutile beauté

My lover's wife and I recognized each other at the cash register at Shoppers Drug Mart. She was buying Q-Tips. I don't remember what I was buying. We made small talk. She looked tired and harried, and I compared myself to her. Though I was completely sleep-deprived and behind on everything, I was radiant, thanks to the ministrations of her husband.

After she'd paid and left, I tried out being angry at her, at the institution of marriage and the precepts of monogamy. What would a society be like in which women weren't expected to respect laws of possession for each other? Why did I have to tone down my desire and my attractiveness so as to not threaten the tired grumpy wife's ownership of the passive object of her husband? Why was it that those of us who saw through the charade of marriage were expected to respect it?

Any outsider would immediately take her side as the wronged one. She, after all, had the culture behind her; she was a faithful wife whereas I was an adulteress and a liar. I was a social pariah, who had deliberately done battle against an institution which was unquestionable. Didn't I know he was *married*? Didn't I know *I* was? Yeah, but what about the lie on which these propietary institutions are founded?

My outrage didn't really work. She was an intelligent beautiful woman who was putting up with her husband's absences and his evasions because of a complex web of household and children and career and family. She may have been practicing her own version of denial in not admitting to herself that her husband had something going on, but it was a whole lot more mature and responsible than his selfish escapism. He and I were doing nothing radical; we were just running away.

One night I cuddled up with my sons on the couch and we watched *Casablanca*. One brown and one blonde head leaned against my shoulders, and the black dog draped herself across us. Near the end, Ingrid Bergman stands between the two men — Humphrey Bogart, her dark and brooding true love, and Paul Henreid, her staunch and kind husband. They both ask her to stay with them, and she's torn as she looks from one to the other. As he burrowed his greasy fingers into the popcorn bowl on my lap, dark-haired Sebastian said, with a musing tone beyond his years, "It's hard to be a beautiful woman."

I thought of myself and my beautiful friends. Most of us are white, educated, middle-class, and endowed with so much privilege that our lives should be a piece of cake. Why did Sebastian's words resonate so much? I took inventory of some of our situations: One friend had been having a long-term affair for years but decided to have her second child by her husband instead of her lover. Another got pregnant by a guy she had a quick affair with, and never told her husband or child. Another was trying to decide between the handyman and her academic husband.

Another was so hungry for sweetness and physical intimacy from her cold husband that she had drunk unprotected sex that gave her conservative spouse a sexually transmitted disease. Another had decided to be a good wife and mother and was having severe headaches and IBS as she swallowed her anger and put up with his laziness, his selfishness, and his smoking. Another had gone back to her first love, women, after getting two beautiful children out of her workaholic husband. Another used the weekends that her partner was out of town to go online and get the kinky sex she couldn't ask him for.

In *Minima Moralia,* one of Theodor Adorno's aphorisms is about *L'inutile beauté,* or "Useless Beauty." He says:

> Women of exceptional beauty are doomed to unhappiness. Even those favoured by every circumstance, who have birth, wealth, and talent on their side, seem as if hounded or obsessed by the urge to destroy of themselves and all human the relationships they contract.[31]

I saw us beautiful women attracted to men who would become intense and passionate about us. We couldn't resist them, though when we were enamored we couldn't sleep, we couldn't eat, we were slowly killing ourselves. But it was so addictive, so exciting!

I saw us beautiful women talking to the brilliant men. We allowed them to explain things to us. The men abstracted, intellectualized, argued, and asserted. We were somewhat hesitant with our ideas. We smiled when we spoke. We allowed ourselves to be interrupted. We listened when others spoke. We lilted the intonation of our voices so that our statements ended with a question mark. We smoldered with all the things we wanted to say.

I saw us beautiful women being mad and mean. Like Brer Rabbit, who gets caught and says, "Do anything to me except please, please, don't throw me in the briar patch!" We knew that our safe spot was actually in the bed that we pretended to resist. As long as we could keep our thick skins on, we wouldn't feel the thorns. We could imagine that we were right where we wanted to be.

When we were alone with each other, we talked and agreed and commiserated. Manic and anxious, we were angry at the men we had chosen and the limits of our lives. We imagined that another man or another situation would be better.

I hated that we were all so unhappy. I never knew what to say when we would have these long intimate conversations, how much to encourage the fantasies of how things could be different. We nodded and murmured, "I hear you.... I know what you mean.... Me too."

Basically the question that we were asking — "This one or that one?" — was the wrong one. We continued to believe that we deserved something that we couldn't quite get, that there was someone out there who knew what it was and who could give it to us. The messier questions that we avoided were perhaps the ones that would have gotten us out of this dilemma: Why do I think that this person or object could satisfy me? How can I begin to accept that I don't know the answers? And that no one else does either?

We weren't stupid, we were just all of a generation that was shaped by the idea that we were entitled to make choices about our lives. That's what mainstream '80s feminism had told us: that we were articulate, proactive, and self-assured agents of our own lives. It was an important message: that our sex lives and choices were our own, and that we were entitled to have the things we wanted. Very different from the messages that the women's world of my mother's generation experienced.

It isn't wrong to question the institution of marriage. Nor is it wrong to act on your desire and fuck whoever you want. But when I was doing that, I was flailing out as an individual who thinks that she's freely making her own choices. I couldn't see myself as part of a larger structure. Even though the other beautiful women were flailing too, I kept getting caught up in the particulars of each story. The larger dynamic of women's precarity, sexism, and affective immaterial labour under which we all suffered was so omnipresent that I couldn't see how it kept us trapped in marriages and situations we hated. As if the only options were Bogey or the nice husband. As if all the beauty that I saw in my friends and myself all funneled itself into one useless false choice.

Dora and the Door

The graduate students in Comparative Literature invited me to be a keynote speaker at their conference. I gave a talk called "Unafraid of the Odium: Psychoanalysis and the Long Novel as Expanded Forms," in which I compared the novels that I had been teaching to the psychoanalysis I was undergoing. It felt like a big public disclosure, to stand in front of colleagues and students and talk about the analysis. I did it in theoretical terms, tying it to a discussion of literature, so as to veil the risk that I was taking.

The title came from Thomas Mann's introduction to *The Magic Mountain*, in which he asks: "When was a story short on diversion or long on boredom simply because of the time and space required for the telling? Unafraid of the odium of appearing too meticulous, we are much more inclined to the view that only thoroughness can be truly entertaining."[32]

What attracted me to Mann's novel is that not much *happens* in it. The plot is negligible compared to the meticulous thinking, reading, talking, observing, and musing that fill the many pages. This is a new form of entertainment, as Mann would have it, in which both author and reader are unafraid of the odium of thoroughness. My hunch about this new form was that it is connected to psychoanalysis, which emerged at the same time. The Modernist long novel responded to and was shaped by the unconscious as a topic, an image, a focus in and of itself.

In his discussion of *The Magic Mountain*, one of my graduate school professors, Fredric Jameson, writes about "the special kind of addiction that must necessarily attach us to the reading of these endless pages."[33] What is the addiction? It's not, as in a page turner, to know what happens. But it hooks us nevertheless. In my presentation, I suggested that we could approach that question about reading by asking another, about psychoanalysis: what keeps the analysand going back, day after day, to lie on a couch and speak to an invisible interlocutor in a disjointed intensely intimate way? Why, when the subject matter can be painful, boring, and repetitive, and the form frustrating and incoherent, does she continue for years?

It has to do, I said, with the relationship between the analyst and the analysand. The analyst keeps the analysand sufficiently hystericized to keep him or her coming back, wanting to access something that she or he believes the analyst knows. To explain what I meant by *hystericized,* I used a quotation of Alain Badiou, in which he describes the hysteric as saying, "Truth speaks through my mouth, I am here. You have knowledge, tell me who I am."[34] The hysteric will reject the analyst's answers as *not quite right,* too objectifying, too reductive.

The author of the long novel puts himself (I use the male pronoun since I was talking about Mann, Proust, and Joyce) in the position of the analyst who keeps us wanting to come back precisely at those moments of not knowing. But the author is *also* the hysteric who keeps writing because he believes that he speaks truth and hopes that his imagined reader will affirm him in it.

So, how do these authors write these long novels? And how should we read them? "Always hystericize!" I said, which was a jokey riff on Jameson's injunction to "always historicize."[35] What I meant was that both authors and readers maintain the desire for knowledge, and, at the same time, the awareness that the possibilities proliferate endlessly: "Could it be this? It's not quite that.... What if I come at it this way?" As readers, we keep coming back precisely at those moments of not knowing, just as the author tries out the same incidents or topics as if from different camera angles, never pretending to have offered his readers the whole picture.

All that not knowing is what Lacan calls "the dimension of ignorance":

> [I]f the subject commits himself to searching after truth as such, it is because he places himself in the dimension of ignorance — it doesn't matter whether he knows it or not. That is one of the elements making up what analysts call "readiness to the transference.[36]

It is not just the analysand who places himself in this dimension, as Lacan clarifies:

> The analyst's ignorance is also worthy of consideration. [...] He doesn't have to guide the subject to *Wissen*, to knowledge, but on to the paths by which access to this knowledge is gained.[37]

Reader/writer, analyst/analysand: we are all in positions of ignorance, we are all desiring. And all this desire and ignorance keeps us together in this long process of the production of words and meanings. This is what psychoanalysis is: "a dialectic, [...] *an art of conversation*."[38]

Instead of telling the audience about my own experience of psychoanalysis, I used a tongue-in-cheek description by Slavoj Žižek: "One of them lies on the couch, stares into thin air and throws out disconnected prattle, whereas the other mostly stays silent and terrorizes the first by the weight of his oppressive mute presence."[39] If that's what analysis is like, I asked, what does Lacan mean when he calls it, echoing Montaigne, "an art of conversation"? It felt as mismatched as when Mann used the word "entertaining" to defend *The Magic Mountain*. Yet just as Mann's thoroughness does hold us within its pages, so too Lacan's dialectic proposes a kind of listening and speaking that is indeed an art of conversation. It's not a dialogue like any other because the analyst is not there to understand, to commiserate or to support. Rather, he is someone upon whom the analysand can project her desires. He is inscrutable in much the way that the reader is. The reader remains silent, like a good analyst. Mann and Proust's narrators are relentless in their search for a reader who will know what they mean. But they can never be sure if the reader does know what they mean. Faced with that silence, they create. They go on. And on.

I felt triumphant and articulate the day after giving this very well-received talk. I had talked so knowingly about analysis. I almost wished that Dr. O had been in the audience. At the appointed hour, I walked into his basement and put my bag down in its usual place, in front of the bookcase. Glancing up, I saw that, behind, the glass, were the complete works of Freud. Had I really never noticed that before? Those pale blue books had been in my direct line of vision from the couch for over two years. I felt dizzy. What I had said in an assured voice to an academic public about psychoanalysis came undone at that moment. I hadn't even known Freud was in the room!

Somewhere, between the pages of one of those books, was the case study that I kept thinking I was going to reread: Dora. Dora is the pseudonym of the 18-year-old girl with hysterical symptoms who, in Freud's interpretation, was in love with her father's friend and jealous of her father's affair. I had read it as an undergraduate, and it had made a huge impression on me. I still had the copious notes in which I'd detailed how much Dora was like me. I knew that there was a feminist critique of Freud's treatment of her and his interpretation of her, but I didn't want to read it, because there was something in Dora's volatility, her sexual excitement, her attraction and repulsion to adults, and her passionate resistance, that resonated with my own experience.

Every now and then Dr. O would bring up Dora, or I would. But then I would say, "I can't. I can't read it yet." I didn't want to have to read a failure of Freud's, in which he misunderstood her and drove her away. I also didn't want to risk finding similarities between Freud and Dr. O, since I had found so many between myself and Dora. And I didn't want to read something that would echo what we were doing every day. I needed us to just continue to do, without recourse to a literary precursor.

Even though I was trained in critical theory, I had never really been interested in psychoanalytic theory as applied to literature or culture. And now it seemed that to read about psychoanalysis would cause me to seek resemblances and interpretations, and to predict outcomes. I believed very strongly that I shouldn't interfere with the process through studying it. Outside of the space of the analysis perhaps Dr. O and I knew things, but in there we both needed to not know.

After having noticed the books, I lay on the couch the next day and felt newly trapped. I kept looking toward the door, wanting to leave, but feeling sure that I couldn't because it was locked. The only door whose lock I had not tested, it seemed to me, was the bookcase. But I didn't want to open it, not yet. I imagined that one day Dr. O and I would share the self-evident knowledge that was contained in those books and not need to talk about it.

I began to panic because I wanted to leave so much, so I tried to negotiate with him. "I know I'm avoiding something. I promise I'll talk about it if you just let me leave today." He said nothing, and I lay there, silent and immobilized except for my twitching foot. When he finally said, "And that's our time for today," I jumped up and left as fast as I could, walking up the stairs to the outer door. I tried to turn the handle, but it was locked. From the inside. Since I was the only person who had come in since my session started, I must have done it unconsciously when I first arrived. Desperate as I had been to leave, I was also, it seemed, desperate to keep us both locked in there together.

Run, Run, Run If You Can

As I walked to analysis the next day, I had to stop at the McDonalds to use their restroom. As I sat on the toilet with my stomach cramping, I thought, over and over in a sing-song way, "What do I do with Dr. O? What do–I–do?"

It came to me in a very bodily metaphor: I spill my guts. I let it all out. I do doo-doo. I reached into the inner recesses of my body and brought the detritus out into the open. But then, after I was done, I walked out the door and went about my everyday activities. What I expelled and exposed in his office — it wasn't worth thinking about, forgotten, disappeared. Flushed.

Whenever I came in anxious and desperate and said, "What should I do? What should I do?"

Dr. O would say, "Doing instead of thinking...."

I told Dr. O that day that I was getting more and more frustrated. It was so complicated, and I was so confused. I couldn't remember the things I understood in analysis, not when I was out in the real world, hungry for clarity, for attention, for drink, for sex.

"What the fuck do you want me to do? Why don't you help me? Answer me? Tell me how to stop?"

He said, "That's our time for today."

It felt too early, like I had just gotten started. I walked away from the house, and then thought to check the time. He had ended the session ten minutes too early.

The next day, I walked in and lay on the couch, silent. He said nothing. I waited him out. Neither of us spoke for long minutes, and I got madder and madder that he was taking time from me again. Finally, I couldn't stand it, and said, "You let me out early yesterday."

"Yes. Yes, I did. I apologize for that."

Another long pause, and then he said, "I felt that you were trying to devour me."

It was so incongruous, so unexpected, that I immediately cried. How could he have perceived me as menacing towards him, when I had felt so helpless? And if he thought that, how many other people felt that towards me when I expressed my need for them? I must come across to everyone as too much, too devouring, excessive, threatening.

I decided that it really was time for me to understand what "acting out" was. According to Sophie De Mijolla-Mellor, it is "the discharge by means of action, rather than by means of verbalization, of conflicted mental content."[40] It is a form of resistance to remembering something repressed that is stirred up by the psychoanalysis. Instead of bringing that repressed memory into words, which is what the analysis is supposed to do, the analysand acts out in an attempt to not remember, but to repeat.

In his essay, "Remembering, Repeating, Working-Through," Freud discusses acting out as a predictable behavior that occurs within psychoanalytic transference and resistance. Because of this, he insists that it be contained within the space of the session:

> Acting out in reality could have grave consequences, precipitating disasters in the patient's life and dashing any hope of cure through psychoanalysis. It is thus up to the analyst, relying on the patient's transference-based attachment, to control the patient's impulses and repetitive acts, notably by extracting a promise to refrain, while under treatment, from making any serious decisions regarding professional or love life.[41]

How could acting out be controlled in this way, so that it only occurred in the safety of the analytic session? I printed this paragraph so as to reread it and obsessively show to friends as I asked them, "Do you think this is what I'm doing? How would I know? Do you think my shrink is bad because he didn't extract a promise from me?"

I couldn't bring myself to ask him, but I worried. Why hadn't he, for instance, stopped me from taking on two different administrative directorships during my analysis? Why hadn't made me swear to stay with my husband and forsake the affair? I felt like the Gingerbread man, running and taunting him to catch me if he could. Why wasn't he chasing me fast enough?

I think that, despite Freud's draconian injunctions, Dr. O understood that I did not live in a bubble that allowed the analysis to do its work without tangible effects on the daily structure of my life. There was no ashram of psychoanalysis to which I could retire and find myself unfettered by quotidian matters, or compulsive behaviors, or addictions. I was doing analysis while living my life, and it was having effects that dragged other people into it.

Over time, I began to know when I was acting out versus when I was doing something that came from my truth. Acting out felt different: it had a prickle and an anxious urgency to it; it caused me to ask endless questions, trying to get people's advice and not being able to accept or hear it. Acting out was when I made decisions that were full of flair and resolve and insistent declaration. Like when I tried to preempt the affair, or when I tried to stop it after a couple of months. I was so panicky and strident that I was basically begging to be refused. There was something so delicious in having my insistence broken down.

The decisions that emerged as a consequence of the slow and arduous work of psychoanalysis were quieter, more determined and inexorable. They didn't flare; they persisted, like a steady drip that etched a groove. That groove formed a path that I couldn't avoid. I knew that to stay on it I had to take a big next step.

That step was going to be the saddest one of my life.

PART THREE

Of course it's easy to fear that autobiography merely exposes a bumptious narcissism, reeking with its primordial first person singular. I'm much more struck by something else: the use of these pages, if anything, to aerate, expose, and ideally to disable or "burn out" the potency of certain violent defenses.

— Eve Kosofsky Sedgwick, *A Dialogue on Love*

PART THREE

Rats

David distrusted the city infrastructure, and would have preferred for us to be off-grid, off the sewage system and electricity. We lived in an old house in downtown Toronto, and had no money to retrofit the house, so it wasn't going to happen. He did what he could though. For instance, he tried to compost all our waste in the back garden, even though Toronto has a good composting green bin program. He built a big wooden and mesh box, in which year-old pears or corn cobs would fossilize and harden instead of decomposing into organic soil. After much struggle, he gave up on it, breaking apart the box in a fit of frustration.

The next day he was out of the house, for a change. I took over the kitchen counter at which he usually sat, and spread the notes for my seminar. Glancing out the back door, I caught a glimpse of scurrying shapes all over the garden. A shudder of repulsion ran through me even before I understood what I was seeing: large rats picking through the refuse from the broken box, the sun catching their shiny fur and pale paws. I knew there were rats around, since we'd found traces of them in the basement before, and once the cat had killed one down there, but now here they were in broad daylight. I tried to concentrate on my work, but every time I caught a glimpse of their movements, I was drawn to watching them, fascinated and horrified.

In analysis, I couldn't stop talking about rats. I remembered the battle between the rats and the Nutcracker. "I'm like Clara, because I wanted to be saved by a handsome nutcracker, but the Rat King wins."

Dr. O drily corrected me, "It was the Mouse King in the ballet."

Rat King, Rat King... why had I said that? Where had I heard that? I went home and googled it, and wished I hadn't (don't do it if you're easily repulsed—the image on Wikipedia is gruesome). A Rat King is a swarm of rats whose tails have become inextricably tangled. The mass happens through a matted mess of blood or feces. The harder each rat tugs to escape the others, the faster the knot will become. The king is not one rat in power, but rather an agglomeration of intertwined rats.

I began my analysis with stories of entrapment and captivity. These tales had an undercurrent of erotic frisson to them, since they fantasized possession and the twisted privilege of being the captor's special chosen one. Now, though, my fears had become more primal and embodied. The writhing rats, all entangled with each other, felt like the enmeshed tangle of marriage and affair and family that I was in at that moment. Only through cutting away their tails could the rats be extricated from their knotted fate. I imagined the swarm snarling and snapping at the knife that was enacting such a brutal but necessary excision.

When I went into Dr. O's office the next day, I described what I had found through shudders and tears. I was deeply repulsed as I lay there, conjuring images of conjoined rats. But I knew I had to keep talking. There were words pushing to the surface that I couldn't bring myself to say for almost the entire session. I could hear their repetitive chant in my head, but they wouldn't come out of my mouth. Finally, scared that the session would end and I would be strangled by the words tangled around my vocal chords, I blurted out, "I want to kill myself."

As soon as I said it, I knew that it was true and not true: "It's not a will to die so much as a desperate will to survive. But to survive I'll have to kill a part of myself."

Dr. O didn't accept this rationalizing caveat. It reduced the force of my pronouncement too much. "Could you," he asked, "allow yourself to acknowledge that you have a destructive, gnawing, suicidal despair?"

I said, "The rats are indeed formed into a King. They reign in my psyche."

Over the next weeks, I was drawn to another myth, the story of the Pied Piper. The piper is the man who is hired to get rid of a village's rats. He performs the task successfully by luring them with music to the banks of the river, into which they jump and drown themselves. But then the ungrateful people refuse to pay the piper, having already forgotten what a plague had been upon them. That night he plays another tune, one so seductive and enchanting that all the children leave their beds and follow him, never to return to their homes.

I was looking for ways to free myself of the rats, but feared the indebtedness or retribution that would come if I got someone to do it for me. I had used David as my salvation to extricate me from the knotted tangles of my family of origin. And I had used a lover as an escape from the terrors of psychoanalysis and the morass of my marriage. Each time I did, I was abdicating responsibility for ridding myself of my gnawing terrors, and I endangered the vulnerable, tender, child-like parts of me that resided alongside the rats.

It was a welter of selves that constituted my self. I had to get in there myself, and untangle each knot, because I couldn't risk forfeiting the precious parts that I no longer wanted to give away. I was so tired of begging the Piper to do it for me, and paying his gouging price.

At the Beginning

Was I really in love, or was the affair just a way of running away from the analysis? There will never be a simple answer to such a question, because there is no pure falling in love, unaffected by other habits and memories and pressures. These contingencies have little to do with the person at hand. And there is no pure psychoanalysis that can be disengaged from the vicissitudes of a life over a period of five years.

I did know that despite my intentions to end the affair, I kept falling into the fantasy that I wasn't being hurt if I was being fucked. That it was the opposite: that I was being loved. To be embodied sexually was so much easier, more familiar, than to be embodied in the discomfort of the analysis. The analysis was going so badly, making so little sense to me. I kept holding my breath during sessions, relieved to just not have to be carrying on the working of living for those static seconds.

One day, when I kept hyperventilating and blanking out, Dr. O said, "At the beginning of analysis, things start coming up that are hard to hold, to look at, and so it's easier to turn to the other."

I couldn't believe that he said "at the beginning" when I had been going for almost three years. What had we been doing all that time if I had just barely begun? It felt like he was making a mistake. I had done so much work already. I had talked and begun to see the importance of certain stories as foundational patterns in my life. Those stories and my interpretation were powerful and convincing. I must be at least halfway through this process.

When I complained of this to a friend, she reminded me of Philip Roth's *Portnoy's Complaint*. The whole novel is a stream of consciousness monologue by an extremely articulate and self-aware narrator. It ends its many pages of rant and ramble with the response by the psychoanalyst: "So [*said the doctor*]. Now vee may perhaps to begin. Yes?"[42]

Like Portnoy, I was articulate. Perhaps suspiciously articulate. The stories that I was telling Dr. O were heartfelt and powerful tales of my childhood, yes, but they were a little too pat. They had a narrative arc that often achieved some kind of closure. I told them in ways that allowed for easy interpretation.

Now, however, I was getting to another place in the stories. I was hitting up against unsayable things, resistances that stemmed from trying to bring into words preverbal terrors of loss or hunger or abandonment. It terrified me to confess the coping strategies I had developed as a small child: the erotic fantasies, the dissociative splitting. If I brought them into language, I would have to give them up.

"Do you think," I asked Dr. O, "that I'm running away running away from the analysis by taking my excess elsewhere?"

He said, "A splinter remains, undetected."

"A splendor?"

"Splendor?"

"I thought that's what you said," I laughed. "I do think of my too-muchness as having a certain splendor. It's vibrant and energetic. I assert it to separate from my family. I'm clinging to the affair and to my anger at David because, even though they keep me blanked out in here, they also make me feel alive. Without them, what would be left of me?"

He didn't respond. I cast my eyes around his office, saying, "Without them, I'll be as smooth as that polished wooden vase on your windowsill. I'll be as empty as it. Better to stay in the marriage *and* continue the affair."

In a session a few days later, he again brought up my not having begun: "Perhaps you fear that if you really begin the analysis you will lose the power to talk? You are good at talking."

"You sound like my mother, who always said I talk too much."

I felt ashamed that I had been talking at him, weaving tales, manipulating stories in order to convince him to care for me. I felt tired. Tired of that fog of shame and the outbursts that would ensue from it. I had asked him whether he cared so many times in so many ways. It was a loud energy-sucking question. Was there something else that it was drowning out with its noisy panic?

As I lay there quietly, the fog began to clear and a more primal fear emerged. The breath caught in my throat as I blurted out, "I'm scared that analysis is exposing me. It's peeling back my skin, and it's going to reveal that I am empty inside. If I don't keep doing, I will be no-body. There will be no one in this room."

This seems, in retrospect, to have been the moment that the analysis began. Or maybe when it came closer to its end, according to this explanation that Lacan gives analysts: "The subject […] begins analysis by speaking of himself without speaking to you, or by speaking to you without speaking of himself. When he can speak to you about himself, the analysis will be finished."[43]

I had been speaking about myself without speaking to Dr. O. All the transference I had done, putting him in imagined positions of authority and knowledge and power, they were not moments of speaking *to him*. When I say "speaking to him," I don't mean that I should have been having a conversation with Dr. O about his personal details or life, but rather that I was not talking to him about what we were doing in that room together.

Now, I was beginning to talk about what the analytic relationship was and did. Instead of starting with "I," many of my comments directly addressed Dr. O by beginning with "you." In a more standard therapeutic narrative, perhaps this would be the moment in which my resistance would end. That wasn't the way it worked in real life, however. I would speak to Dr. O about myself, then fall back into projecting onto him, then realize, then blank out again. It was like relapsing back into an addiction, to that delicious feeling of abdication and empty-headedness that meant I was done for that day. That I wasn't going to *know* the things I didn't want to know.

That's why, I think, psychoanalysis takes such a long time. By the end of the five years, I had come to terms with the fear, pain, and desire that had me acting out in such destructive ways. But my awareness of those negative affects emerged in small increments. I only saw as much as I could possibly bear at any given moment. It was like getting a glimpse of something through a swinging door that opens and shuts. Those glimpses came from allusions, dreams, or impulses that exposed the darker sides of my desires. On the couch, I experienced the plenitude of my conscious and unconscious motivations and counter-demands. I saw the ways that I unwittingly sabotaged what seemed to be in my own best interest. Then the door would swing shut again, and I would go home and carry on with "normal" life.

PART THREE

Blanking Out

The subway train kept stopping on the tracks, which meant that I was going to be late. I tried to block out the irritation, be calm and cool, not feel that I was a victim to its stops and starts. When I arrived and told Dr. O about it, he said, "Blocking things out?"

I knew that he was talking about how I would go blank in the middle of feeling too much. But I was irritable, and said, "Yes, like the train, analysis does stop and start and go too fucking slowly."

He didn't respond. I really wanted to goad him, to get him to admit how hard this was on me. I continued, "What would it be like if, just once, you could say, 'Don't worry, it's normal, everyone blanks out'? I mean, I know that it must be true, but I could use some reassurance every now and then. Sometimes you're too hard for me. You expect me to swallow huge truths and realizations. You should give me smaller spoonfuls."

He said, "It's hard to know how best to care for and protect a fragile delicate thing."

At first I thought he was mocking me, like I was pleading for some kind of special treatment.

But then he said, "How do you feed a lamb that has lost its mother?"

An inchoate darkness descended over me. I recognized it as the same feeling I had experienced before when he tried to get me to talk about my mother not breastfeeding me. That time, I had been resistant since it sounded too self-helpy. I wasn't interested in some "inner child" story about being deprived of the breast. Now, though, it felt like a fundamental lack that I had spent my whole life trying to fill.

I told him that it was weird that he had brought up babies because I hadn't slept the previous night worrying that I was pregnant. "Let me be clear," I said, "I'm not *actually* anxious about being pregnant. So there's no need for us to talk about it."

"You want to make me aware that you're anxious without me taking the baby the way you were taken?"

"No, it's a red herring. I want you to know something about my anxiety, which has chosen a baby as its distracting object."

I finished the session by saying that if I was pregnant, I would never leave this baby.

As the days went by, my period was still late. It wasn't going to come, it seemed, until I made myself think about it all. Not whether I wanted a baby or not, but whether I had been wanted as a baby. So I tried to imagine myself as a baby wanting her mother. Immediately, I blanked out. It felt good, so high and light in my head. It was like catching a nap when you know you should be on watch for something. Just a quick little shut eye, even if you'll regret it later.

Analysis was like an anchor, though. It continued to pull me down into that darkness that I wanted to avoid. The next day, I got a very strong image of the container that I continued to seek. It was my mother's womb, but in it I was an intruder, growing bigger despite her. It seemed so clear: *She hadn't wanted me.* I went dark and blank.

I said, "It doesn't work for me anymore, to think of myself as either puppet master or puppet. As agent or victim. I don't want us to just see me as a victim, someone who acts the way she does because she wasn't wanted. I don't want us to forgive my actions because I lacked maternal love."

This was the circle I couldn't square. I was trying to measure how much I, as an individual, should take responsibility for who and what I was, versus how much I should blame on histories and structures that were beyond my control. For what should I hold myself accountable? And for what should I forgive myself?

The Dwarves

David and I were watching the television show *In Treatment*. It was a good way to be together without having to talk. The little time that we spent with each other was otherwise tense. We argued about politics, finances, the children, the house; everything except for what was really going on, that I was distanced and withdrawn, that we weren't having sex, that I was rarely home.

In Treatment gets the closest I've seen on television to representing some of the dynamic of the psychoanalytic session, engaging as it does with representations of transference, dissociation, denial, resistance, and acting out. It doesn't, of course, replicate the long duration, which is the most fundamental aspect, but it makes for good watching, and Gabriel Byrne is charming as a conflicted analyst.

The character that most stands out for me is an articulate woman named Mia. In one of the episodes, she says, "I'm impossible.... I'm demanding, I'm needy, I'm angry, and I'm weepy. I'm the seven fucking dwarves." She delineates the contradictory and disparate aspects of herself as a hodgepodge of characters that all mill around inside her, demanding that she not suppress or ignore them.

The boys and I had recently watched the 1937 Disney *Snow White*, in which the dwarves — Grumpy, Bashful, Dopey — personify different affects. Snow White's name comes from her mother's wish for a child who embodies opposites: white as snow, black as ebony. In the Disney version, Snow White is not stark black and white, but drawn with a warmth of hues. Like light and shadow falling across snow, her edges are not distinct. It was a stroke of brilliance on the part of Disney to have named the dwarves after the negative attributes that the purely good girl does not have.

Snow White is an animated human figure and the dwarves are figures of animated affect, caricatures and embodiments of that which she cannot hold within her. They trip and dance around her in their various animations like tamed versions of the spirits in Pandora's box. In the little wooden house, a haven from the dark woods in which she was abandoned, all aspects emerge and demand to be held in the foreground. Even the evil of the wicked witch takes place within the house. She leans across the fluid threshold between interior and exterior, and proffers her poisoned apple. Love/hate, masculine/feminine, beautiful/ugly;

all jostle across the foreground. It is not possible to maintain a singular meaning, position, or identity.

Watching this reminded me of Lacan's comments on Hans Holbein's painting, *The Ambassadors*.[44] The painting portrays important people surrounded by emblems of wealth and power, but across the painting there's a stain that juts across the rich rug at the base of the scene. Looked at head-on it is a grey smear of paint that seems extrinsic to the painting. Looked at sidelong, however, a skull emerges. This anamorphic image changes the whole painting. It is a *memento mori,* a reminder that death equalizes all worldly differences of class and prestige. Gazing at the painting on the internet, at this moment of my analysis, I read it as a reminder of the powerlessness and unknowability at the heart of ourselves, over which we try, and fail, to assert our power and knowledge.

Lacan talks about the pleasure of "seeing its emergence from an indecipherable form."[45] He's right, I think. It functions the way that psychoanalysis was functioning for me: to show a thing that was always right there, ignored but present in the commonplace understanding, the obvious story. In terms of my own version of hysteria, I began to see the smear — gray, dark, hidden — as the raw demand that I made on others to tell me what I needed to know. Its darkness made the colors of seduction and desire brighter. I felt so alive in my restless urges to seduce and destroy. I may have wished I could stop, but every time I felt the little tug of a fish hooked by a seductive question, I was hooked myself.

Like a deluded viewer who only attends to the details in the painting, I had been missing the smear that cut across my life story. That smear was my desire, the demanding too muchness that led me to seek and to hurt. I feared that excess, but it also made me feel alive. Now, however, I was learning to look more closely, even though desire is not something that can be looked at head on. First I had to notice the way it jutted into the image of my life, and then look at it sidelong, knowing that it would never be fully visible, and that it is as terrifying as a death's head.

Caught up in trying to gain people's love, in trying to choose who I wanted, I hadn't ever interrogated my belief that someone or something could fix my dissatisfaction. That belief had begun to crumble as I looked, with curiosity and dispassion, at the urgent demands and fears that had driven me to act as I had all my life. I could sometimes catch a glimpse of the fact that I was flawed, imperfect, multiple. That I was the seven fucking dwarves *and* Snow White.

Drift

I sat in the waiting room. Waiting. He must be tied up, I thought, with his previous analysand. He never runs overtime with me. Why would he give that person extra time? But there are no shoes outside the door. Perhaps the analysand is wearing them. Or maybe Dr. O isn't there. Maybe he has forgotten about our time today. But he's never forgotten. Something must have happened to him. Would someone call me if he's sick? What if he's dead?

The minutes passed and I tried to keep my breathing calm, distracting myself by reading the titles of books on his shelves. I was getting more and more certain that he was dead, and wondered what I was supposed to do. Just go home and wait for a phone call? Not admit to whoever called that I had been waiting there for him, while he lay dead behind the closed door? I hated that I was so anxious. I wanted to talk to someone about it, but the only person I could think of to tell these insanely exaggerated thoughts was my shrink. Who had now died on me.

Fifteen minutes later, the door opened and he stood there, looking pale and truly apologetic. He said he had been caught up dealing with something and had lost track of the time. I said it was okay, no problem, and went in and lay there in silence for twenty minutes. Finally, I told him that I had been sure that he had died. Just as I began to get at my underlying fear of abandonment, he said, "And that's our time for today."

The next day, I lay down, and he asked if I could stay an extra fifteen minutes to make up for the time lost. I couldn't believe that he was offering me extra time. Then he said, "You were not mistaken in thinking about death. I was busy dealing with the fallout from a colleague's unexpected death."

This was one of the most surprising and delightful things about Dr. O. Serious and inflexible as he seemed, he believed that we both swam in an unconscious soup when we were in a session. We heard things that were unsaid, and sometimes anticipated each other's next words. It was companionable, the way we would startle each other by saying something that the other had been about to say.

I later read Freud's essay, "Recommendations to Physicians Practicing Psycho-Analysis," in which he says,

> the attitude which the analytic physician could most advantageously adopt was to surrender himself to his own unconscious mental activity, in a state of *evenly suspended attention,* to avoid so far as possible reflection and the construction of conscious expectations, not to try to fix anything that he heard particularly in his memory, and by these means to catch the drift of the patient's unconscious with his own unconscious.[46]

I needed Dr. O to make mistakes like forgetting that I was waiting out there. They always tickled me, even if they also scared me. His slips subverted the position of authority in which I placed him as someone who knew something that he would tell me in due time. Instead, they placed him alongside me as we navigated these unknown waters. Me and Dr. O, drifting along in the murk of our unconsciouses. Not mine, not his, but something we had created together.

PART THREE

How the Mighty Are Fallen

A woman I knew complained about her husband to me. She said that the thing that absolutely repulsed her was neediness, that she couldn't stand to have a man cling to her. I pointed out, having seen her with him, that she herself seemed to rely tremendously on him, even as she disparaged him. She said that she knew she was needy, but she still hated it when it was reciprocated.

At a dinner party later, I watched her belittle her husband, interrupting him to correct his stories, rolling her eyes at his comments. When she talked, she was charming and expressive, and he listened to her with a smile on his face. He so obviously adored her. She knew he did, and didn't intend to say such mean things to him, but couldn't stop herself. Both of them would look so pained when she did, like they couldn't stand the appearance of this ugliness in something that was so sweet between them.

He would never leave her. She couldn't believe her good luck that he stayed, but she also despised him for it. Couldn't he see how vicious she was? How could anyone be stupid enough to just stick around? I so recognized this irresistible urge to ridicule, humiliate, reject, and despise an adored and admired man. She had told me that she, like me, had a father who paid little attention to her. Now, as a beautiful woman, she was capable of gaining the attention of many men. But she had chosen one, and allowed herself to love him. So here she was, in a position of vulnerability that was too reminiscent of her relationship with her father. She couldn't help but try her best to topple him.

I saw in her eyes the need that would turn to contempt. And I saw myself do the same thing.

I saw the wreck of my lover's life when we came to the end of the affair. That night that he wanted me to stay with him as he sniffled and coughed. He said, "My mother always used to pat my back when I was sick," and I rolled my eyes in the dark.

I saw him fantasize about a life together with me and I shuddered at the thought of having to wake up every morning to his petty worries.

I saw him drink himself into a falling down stupor, and I walked away sober.

I saw him lose a battle at work and be talked about behind his back, and I listened for all the sordid details.

I saw him accused of sexual harassment by students, and realized, with a clarity that sickened me, that I had thought his flirty attention, way back when I first met him, was directed at me, whereas it was just how he was with women.

I saw him panic when his wife went out of town and he had to take care of his children, and I thought, "What kind of father is he?"

I saw him sob as I was cold and distant towards him, and I hated him for his excessive emotion.

I saw him groan in ecstasy the last time he came inside me, and I thought he was gullible and easily pleasured.

I saw him beg his wife to take him back after he had lost both me and her, and when she refused him, I thought, "Good for her!"

And when I said all these things to Dr. O, he said, "How the mighty are fallen!"

That hit me hard. I had raised my lover up on a pedestal and then toppled him off of it, making sure that there was no way he could erect it again. Why did I have such a wish to destroy, to bring so much pain to others and to myself? Pain — the acute suffering of a broken heart or broken expectations — felt so real. But it was starting to seem like the easy way out.

The singer Courtney Barnett gets it right with the lyric, "Don't put me on a pedestal, I'll only disappoint you."[47] The warning is also a demand: don't ascribe characteristics to me that I can't live up to. And yet… it is so thrilling to be admired, and to admire. How could a man resist the vision that I had of him, when I invited him to stand up on the high pedestal I had erected for him, making him feel that I saw something in him that no one had ever seen before. Something he very much wanted to be. And that I wanted him to be.

Loving men was my resistance to the process of psychoanalysis. Obsession takes up a whole lot of energy. Sex is distracting. I was addicted to the cycle of giving myself away into love.

The compulsion to repeat seemed unavoidable, and I wondered for the first three years of analysis whether it would be yet another scene of this fundamental act in my life, whether I would give myself to Dr. O. Despite the Freudian predictions of transference, however, I never fell in love with my psychoanalyst. Instead, I dragged the other loves into the analysis so that I could bring them into language, hear the constant refrains that circulated in my mind — "maybe he's the one," "dropped with indifferent beak," "I want to kill myself."

To listen to these phrases was to begin to understand how formative they were to my sense of self and others. But now analysis was pushing me to not repeat the same pattern over and over again. All the drama around the affair, around tangled love, was becoming increasingly irrelevant, the path of least resistance. It wasn't the make-or-break factor of my life. My symptom of "I don't know, but I act" seemed more important. To do so as to not face responsibility of having to *be* with something, to face it, understand its meaning.

Dr. O said that I seemed to be on the verge of being able to talk instead of just doing. I felt a leap of recognition and agreement, and began to agree by giving him an example of my new ability. But then I stopped myself, and told him I didn't want to share that story as if we were two rational adults talking together about the remarkable effects of psychoanalysis.

He said quietly, "Don't want to risk having hope?"

My Other Half

In Philip Pullman's *The Golden Compass,* the characters are linked symbiotically to a "daemon," which takes on the shape of different animals and stays close to the human at all times. Humans and daemons are distinct individuals who sometimes argue or contradict each other, but they are also so interconnected that they feel each other's fear or excitement.

The villains in the novel engage in cruel experiments in which they attempt to harness the energy released when the force field between a child and its daemon is severed. The results are devastating: "A human being with no daemon was like someone without a face, or with their ribs laid open and their heart torn out."[48] The amputated children are left limp and pathetic, frantically searching and stumbling, thrown off balance by the lack of their daemon. They die shivering and moaning the name of their other half.

I told Dr. O about this magic of having another being who is always with you, not too close but never absent. I shuddered with shallow-breathed fear as I imagined what it would be like to have that bond cut. It made me think about Siamese twins who share organs and the boundedness of uninterrupted flesh, and the awful feeling of phantom limb/twin that must come at the price of a surgically gained individuality.

I knew what I feared so much about these images of separation. It was that they made me think of my daemon David, inextricably bound to my heart, my mind, my body. What animal would he — tall, lanky, shaggy, sweet, angry, volatile, earthy, raw — be? Maybe a Chewbacca to my reckless Harrison Ford-ish behavior. Coming to the rescue when I'd gotten myself in too deep, ready to embark on whatever outlandish idea I had. Mutely expressive, and unconditionally devoted.

We were together for so long, so in love, so cathected onto each other. Wouldn't I bleed if we surgically excised each other? How could I untangle the Rat King without cutting away some vital part? When I was with David, I felt that I could be flawed, mean, insecure, stupid. I felt so secure in his love, I didn't anxiously try to keep it. I had never felt that comfortable with anyone before. It was only when we were together that I could be myself. Analysis was making me question, however, what "myself" even was.

When Dr. O asked if I was scared to risk hoping that the analysis was changing me, he was right. I was scared to hope for change because what was emerging, inexorably, was that I had to look at my marriage. I didn't like what I would most likely see; that I needed to end it, even though it could kill me to do so. Because it was also killing me to stay. I was so split and anxious and destructive, juggling like a maniac in order to keep it all up in the air. How could I feel hope that I was gaining self-knowledge, if that knowledge would lead me to sever the bond that was definitional to who I was and what I did?

I said to Dr. O, "I can't talk anymore, I have a headache."

"A splitting headache?" he asked. I nodded in dumb and teary agreement.

"How much," he continued, "don't you want to talk about what you want, that you will even split your head to avoid it?"

I cried more.

"Do you think I'm forcing you? That I want something from you? That I want to know?"

I paused, and then said," I think it's more that we've entered into a contract. We both want to know."

"Hmm.... A part of you doesn't."

Dr. O was not the villain who would excise part of me. But talking with him was forcing me to do the math, and it was coming up short. My usual equation had been 1+1=1. David and I were one unit. The problem lay, I recognized, in that we were not each a full 1, but rather a ½. Each of us giving half of ourselves, and not demanding more. Perhaps we both wanted to give more, get more, but we couldn't do it with each other.

To split from David would leave me halved. To think about this was as difficult for me as understanding a physics formula of divisions, of fissions, of fusions. What I knew is that I didn't know how to divide and come out whole.

Ever After

I walked into the basement after having lunch with Cheryl, a colleague who confided in me her latest extramarital transgressions. Every time we met she'd tell me about who she'd slept with, and then rehearse the two options available to her: stay with her husband or follow her impulses.

I used to find her so fascinating in all her dark anger and restlessness. Her frustration with her partner, her desire for someone and something else: they resonated with my own dissatisfaction and my continuous seesawing "this one or that one?" Today, though, I was tired of her. So much drama, so much urgency—about what? I would have preferred to talk about our children, or work, or religion, or climate change. "Anything other," I said to Dr. O, "than this binary back and forth between two men."

He said, "Weren't there three ducks?"

I laughed, tickled that he remembered that third duck, with its waggling little tail. I'd described it as provocative, but now it held another valence for me. The choice was not between one or the other of the two cute ducks as they skimmed across the surface. The submerged duckling represented the third option of diving into the murky depths of the unconscious element of psychoanalysis. There, binaries don't hold. The questions aren't about either/or. They are instead, more fundamentally, about what you want. And what you don't want.

To state clearly and simply, "I want this," is no easy feat. That kind of claim risks confrontation. It makes you vulnerable as you let others see your desire, no matter how unacceptable or unseemly it may be. This is what Lacan calls the "ethics of psychoanalysis": to not give ground on your desire.[49] Even though it may be the thing that you most want and need, you so easily forfeit it in the face of fear, pressure, disapproval, guilt, or a feeling of not deserving. And you don't even know that you've forfeited it, because you haven't allowed yourself to know what it is. Psychoanalysis first brings you to the truth of what you want. Then the ethical question is whether you will stay true to that desire.

That night I couldn't sleep. I saw that Liam's light was still on. Even though he was too old for bedtime stories, I went in and asked if I could read to him. He scooted over on his bed, and I pulled the Philip Pullman book of fairy tales off his shelf. I snuggled next to him under the covers, and we chose "Hansel and Gretel."

After the children follow the white pebbles home to the parents who have tried to abandon them, the stepmother insists they take them deeper into the woods again, and the father accedes, because, according to the Pullman version, "If you've given in once, you have to give in ever after."

"That's not true," Liam interrupted.

I stopped reading and looked at him, astonished. How did he, a child, know what I was now learning, that just because you've given in once doesn't mean you need to keep doing it. Hansel and Gretel's father doesn't know it. He abandons his children. Not because he doesn't love them, but because he is split between the conflicting demands of his lover and his children. Between the fantasy of himself as parental provider and the reality of all four of them starving under his roof. That fantasy allows only for a dichotomy. He is *either* the good father who feeds his children *or* the bad father who abandons them.

When his wife insists that they get rid of the children, he chooses the illusion of being in love, just the two of them free of the constraints of family and dependency. I recognized that running away into escapist fantasy. It feels like a third option, but in fact it's just an avoidance of the binary.

I like to imagine that when the children return, they *and* the father have learned something about how willing they were to risk their lives for the false promise of plenty and ease. The three of them will live together in their little house, knowing that the fantasy of an either/or choice is not the solution. They will stay true to the quest of finding what they want and sticking with it.

With all the breathless to-and-fro that I had done all my life, the predominant feeling had been one of indecision and confusion. To feel torn was a continuous reassertion of what I unconsciously believed: that I was *not allowed* to know what I need. Realizing this opened a gentle and gradual transformation in me. It wasn't that I had to be decisive through making conscious choices that kept me on track. It was that I didn't *have to be* confused or divided. That I did actually know what I needed, if I could only permit myself to know.

Bloodlines

I was living half a life, in a half-functioning household, in half a marriage. It was a perpetual civil war, divisions drawn across intimate relationships. It made me think of my parents' families. In the Spanish Civil War, my grandmother had a Republican brother and a Fascist one. On my father's side, the family had produced a Confederate soldier and a Union one during the American Civil War. In both families, the bloodlines were scarred by internal divisions.

Dr. O said, "How do you live in a country, a house, a psyche that is divided?"

"It's even in my name," I said, "grafted together from both sides of my family: Eva for my mother, Evelyn for my paternal grandmother, and Lynn for the sweet girl down the street that my mother liked when she was pregnant with me. The hyphen holds it all loosely together. A hyphen, however, looks like a minus sign. It adds something at the same time as it subtracts. 'Eva-Lynn' doesn't satisfy anyone, not the Spanish speakers for whom 'Lynn' is foreign, nor the English speakers who don't know how to pronounce the 'e.'"

When I was in my twenties and already published under my name, my mother offhandedly suggested I take out the hyphen since it didn't really work. "Too late," I said. Anyway, it worked as well as the whole intercultural marriage between my parents had worked.

Dr. O, who never talked about himself, said, "My first name, Thomas, means twin."

I told him about one of my favorite picture books from when I was little. It was called *The Two Too Twins,* about two young children being told, over and over, by the grownups they want to be near, that they are too much.[50] Too messy, too little, too noisy. At the end of the book, they find out it's their birthday. They are told that they will no longer be "too" because they are two. I liked this, and I think Dr. O did too. The twins are not one, they are two. Two separate individuals. The confluence of them, many-faceted as it is, is not one mess, but two, made by two.

To have a double name or a doubling name afforded us both a handy metaphor for what it means to be a self. To chase after being One — whole, coherent, unified — was a fiction whether I did it with myself or with another. That aspiration to Oneness is what made me feel that I was too much, too messy, too noisy, too clamorous. Thomas and I, we weren't One, we were many.

The next day, I told Dr. O that when I got my first period at age thirteen, I had horrible insomnia. I would lie in bed paralyzed with fear as I imagined a man climbing a ladder into my bedroom. It was a reprise of the Rapunzel story, I guess. I had always allowed Dolores entrance into my chamber, and now here was the man who had found the secret way. But if he was a prince, he was a threatening and terrifying one. He was a man who wanted me so much that he threatened the inviolability of my family's walls to split me off from them. Those walls had always been paper thin anyway, since my family had not seemed to want to protect me and possess me, unlike this man, who was relentless in his pursuit of me.

Dolores would comment on the blood stains in my underwear, whether the blood was bright red or *chuca*. *Chuco* is a Salvadorean word that means dirty, stained, foul. I always thought it was the word you would use to talk about a brackish brown puddle, but maybe that was because if I came in muddy from splashing in one, she would say that I had gotten all *chuca*. It embarrassed me when she said it about my panties, the *chu* rolling from the inside of her mouth into the sharp fricative. I hated how intimate she was with my periods, how there was no way, in my house, to hide your dirty laundry from her. I knew, also, that she mourned my entry into womanhood, and feared that I could get into trouble, like she had.

Dr. O said, "Yesterday there was a difficult point where it seemed like the divided structure of your mind was like a divided house. You spoke of civil war. Today, Dolores emerges as the figure who cleans up the mess, hides the stains."

It made sense to me. Dolores was so often the false third term that would smooth over the dichotomies. A synthesis of my Old World mother and my New World father, she was the repository of all the dirtiness, both physical and emotional.

Then Dr. O said, "Maybe I am your Dolores. Perhaps you see me as just hired help. The unworthy but willing recipient of your brackish streams of consciousness…."

Leave

I got a fellowship from the Jackman Humanities Institute at University of Toronto. It awarded me a six-month teaching leave. Combined with the semester leave that was due to me after three years of teaching, this meant I would, for the first time in my academic life, have a full year off to research and write. I felt certain that, with that amount of time, I would be able to complete the project I had proposed, "Too Much: The Time of Reading, the Time of Psychoanalysis." When I reread the proposal now, I'm fascinated by the disconnect between how knowledgeably I wrote *about* psychoanalysis, while I was such an incoherent mess *in* it. My writing is so self-assured, intimate yet also academic. Here are a few paragraphs from what I proposed:

Too Much is a short book on length. In it I discuss the politics and pleasures of certain long and slow forms of literature, film, and psychoanalysis that seem to run counter to the models of efficiency and brevity that define our society. In a personal and contemplative style, I write about the discomfort that such texts and practices elicit, arguing that they are anxiety-producing because they are perceived as too much: they take too long, they are too introspective, self-absorbed, and perhaps irrelevant. The book is a consideration of ignorance, of anxiety, and of the discomfort of wanting to know. In short, of hysteria as a reading and writing practice. Holding itself to a contained form, it struggles with its fear of being too much at the exact same time as it revels in its drive to too muchness. Its form is that of a paranoid book, trimming any excess because it desperately believes that its argument matters and suspects that if it takes up too many words, no one will listen. It sometimes feels that it should be less earnest so as to be more palatable, but it also loves every word, savoring all its nuance, its delicacy. Thin, it imagines itself fat, worrying and hoping that it will spill out over its container in the way that its subject matter does.

Dilatory and digressive, a novel like Proust's *À la recherche du temps perdu* or Thomas Mann's *The Magic Mountain*, the films of Chantal Akerman or Chris Marker, or the years-long process of psychoanalysis, require a huge expenditure of time. Of time that is spent alone and not alone, attending to what is said and to what is not said, inside an interiority that is terrifying in its obviousness, its inscrutability, its repetition, and its extension. As someone who spends such an extraordinary amount of time on the introspective practices of reading (both literature and cultural texts) and being psychoanalyzed, I am afraid of being self-absorbed, so I strive to be efficient. However, if I am too concise and ordered, I long to be wordier, slower, excessive. Unsure why I struggle between two untenable positions, I believe that there is a way to reconcile them, that there is a way to be too much, to give free rein to desire, and at the same time to be contained, circumspect. The impasse lies, I am coming to suspect, in the spurious ideological promise of synthesis. Our culture seems to promise, if not to cure, at least to manage oppositions or incompatibilities. They can be "worked through" or behaviorally modified or even medicated so as to become less troublesome, less provocative of anxiety. Nowadays, in a culture that defines itself as post-psychoanalysis and post-modern, the friction of these two irreconcilable ways of being in the world are smoothed over. It seems that you can be exactly what you want to be, you can balance excess. You can successfully inhabit a third position that conflates differences, that is neither too much nor too little.

This book is not a lot of things, perhaps worth enumerating. It is not an analysis of the work of Marcel Proust, James Joyce, Sigmund Freud, Chantal Akerman, Chris Marker, or others, nor does it undertake psychoanalytic readings of any of these texts. It engages with all of them in a subjective discussion of the practice of reading and teaching, but it does not talk "about" what happens in them or about their themes or motifs. Rather I want to think about how we read them. About how we don't know. About how when we actually immerse ourselves in these expanded forms, we necessarily change from one discursive position to another, from knowledge to ignorance, from a university discourse to a hysteric's discourse.[51] We tend to forget that there is something strong in not knowing. My book reclaims the space and time of not knowing through its insistence on a reading and writing process that hinges not only upon the moments of insight, but also those of blindness [Paul de Man echo!]. Taking my impetus from the discipline of psychoanalysis, I believe that we can put into words our experience when we engage not only with stories or concepts that we easily grasp, but also with boredom and gaps and repetitions and inscrutability.

Though it still sounds good to me, I never wrote that book. I never wrote the Latin American sound project either. My virtual desk drawers are full of great ideas. But I was way too deep into the *not knowing* that analysis had opened up inside me to write a knowing book.

I didn't talk about this project with Dr. O. I might have talked about a scene in a movie or novel, but I never told him that I had formulated an intellectual argument about what we were doing. He was with me behind the curtain, and would not be duped by the expert way that I discussed the practice of psychoanalysis. It would have been like those moments at dinner parties when David would charmingly tell a story to the other guests about a trip we had taken, and I would be sitting there thinking about all the things he had left out — the arguments, the underwear not packed, the children crying, the flight almost missed because he was yelling at the counter agent.

I didn't talk about the project because I wasn't ever going to do it. And I had something else to talk about, or at least talk *around*: the end of my marriage. I didn't know it yet, but that was how I was going to spend my leave. Not writing. Leaving.

Anti-Revelation

I never knew the moment that my analysis actually "began." It was more that I came to know that I had been doing it. When I look at the analysis as a whole, I see that it was not a straight trajectory, but rather a series of loops in a spiral. I would find myself circling back to the same incident or feeling, repeating it from a different perspective or understanding, sometimes noticing a hitherto insignificant tiny detail, other times seeing it from the macro level. Every time it would have a different valence, and cause me to react with different emotions to it.

I didn't have revelations, the way I had imagined I would. There are still many half-glimpsed shimmers or dark spots that I don't understand. These misses are why the most exciting part of Proust's entire book is, for me, not the famous madeleine moment, in which the taste of the cake in his mouth floods him with memories from his past. Instead, it comes in the second book, *Within a Budding Grove,* where the narrator describes a memory that remains inaccessible. He is a passenger in a carriage as it drives by a hill with three trees on it. The sight fills him with a profound yet incomplete happiness. The trees are familiar, but they seem to conceal something he cannot grasp:

> That pleasure, the object of which I could but dimly feel, that pleasure which I must create for myself, I experienced only on rare occasions, but on each of these it seemed to me that the things which had happened in the interval were of but scant importance, and that in attaching myself to the reality of that pleasure alone I could at length begin to lead a new life.[52]

The carriage moves on. The narrator cannot capture what it is that the trees seem to be urging him to understand. That's it. The scene ends, and never comes up again in the novel.

The narrator, knowing that it is up to him "to create for himself" the pleasure that will allow him to "begin to lead a new life," attempts to understand something that resists being brought into signification. The scene stands out for me because it's so different from conventional narrative. It is contrary to the kinds of epiphanic revelations that Proust himself has established as the stuff of writing. Instead, it maintains a radical lack of closure.

It is very close to a reality of my psychoanalysis. Many of the things I said in the years that I lay on the couch did not rise to the level of full signification. That was, in fact, their full signification. Lacan is perhaps talking about this when he says that "the only way in which to evoke the truth is by indicating that it is only accessible through a half-saying [*mi-dire*], that it cannot be said completely for the reason that beyond this half there is nothing to say."[53]

I thought, again and again, of Alain Badiou's *Ethics*. Badiou talks about the possibility of an event that could interrupt what you think you know about reality, or truth, or yourself. That event — which could be in the realm of politics, or science, or art, or love — demands that you persevere in a commitment to the truth that it has shown you. And the "you" of which it demands commitment is a new subjectivity that has emerged from this encounter.

In the event of psychoanalysis (which, in Badiou's terms, falls under the category of a love event), I was faced with a truth that seized me and broke my sense of myself as stable and knowable. It demanded my fidelity, that I persevere in its radical unknowing. Badiou states it as "do not give up on that part of yourself that you do not know."[54]

This event was not about me, it was about the dyad that Dr. O and I created as a template, a model, for all the other relationships in my past, present, and future. We were in a formal and artificial relationship in which very informal and true things happened. I needed that kind of structured relationship in order to break with the kinds of relationships that I was used to, in which the other person became the Other of fantasy, of completion. The psychoanalytic relationship allowed me to turn the Other into another. I was finding myself *in relation to others.*

As the analysis progressed, my questions became less "Is it this or is it that?" "Am I one thing or another?" and more real inquiries into how to speak into being that which had not been spoken before. Either Dr. O or I could answer these questions, because I was no longer asking him to give me the answers. Instead, it was, "I may already have the answer within me, and I know that talking to you is a way to get closer to it, so I'm posing the question to both of us, since either one could have the answer." That was the Freudian dialectic of psychic transformation. That was the Badiouan perseverance in fidelity to a truth that we didn't fully know.

Hot Water Bottle

By the end of the third year of analysis, my marriage was completely falling apart. Before I left for a conference in Vancouver, I told David that we needed to talk when I returned. I wasn't sure what I wanted us to talk about, but I knew that I didn't want to live in such a lifeless limbo anymore. It was drizzly and overcast when I landed, and there was an email from David entitled "Monday Talking Points." I waited till I was on the Skytrain to downtown to read the long message.

He started by saying that we'd had such a sad winter. We had hit the doldrums that we'd seen in other couples, when we'd thought that they should just split up. The fact that we were not having sex was a big part of this. I thought about the sex I had been having with someone else. I was sickened by how little I'd noticed that he'd been sad all season.

I had seemed friendly the night before I left, he said, when I reached towards him with my foot across Liam, who had come into our bed in the middle of the night. He wrote:

> I had been thinking dark thoughts, but that foot changed things. According to the various states of consciousness with which I related to it, it was variously a tender of love, an earnest of possibilities and, towards morning, a realization that it had never been a foot. It was a hot water bottle I'd heated myself. You must have flipped it over onto me hours before. I've mistaken these rubber bottles for cats and dogs, why not a lover?

The image of him, comforted and encouraged by my warm limb reaching towards him, made me cry on the train. It makes me cry to even write it here. He wasn't a captor or an authority to be evaded. He was my friend and partner and loved bedmate. David had been waiting all that sad winter for me to reach my foot towards him, and I hadn't told him that I didn't want to, that

I couldn't, that I never would again. I hadn't told myself either, though the truth of it was ever more evident.

In our years together, it had usually been up to me to broach difficult topics of conversation. To point out problems between us, to insist that we talk about our relationship. But this year, the year that I had been talking every day in the most unfettered stream-of-consciousness way possible, I hadn't talked to David. Instead, I had used the words that I spoke outside of the analysis to weave webs of erotic seduction around another man. And I had used our sleeping son's body to fill the growing gap between us, so that David wouldn't ask questions about why I wasn't reaching towards him in the night.

I think this was how it had to end. I couldn't have talked to him about my desires and the problems in our marriage because words were our illusion and our downfall. We had spoken so many. David and I were both skilled in language, and when we talked, it felt like no one could talk the way we did, like we had something exceptional and unique and irreplaceable. I didn't want to rekindle that, because I had come to distrust it. To cling to the idea of our exceptionality was a way to ignore all the things that didn't work in our daily lives. I was tired of all the glass castles, the weaving of webs.

I was exhausted by pronouncements. Made by me, by men. Declarations of love and intention that were at odds with what happened in our daily lives. It reminded me of what my father would say on the rare occasions when he would scoop me onto his lap: "I love you more than you love me." I never knew how to respond to that. I didn't know how much he loved me. But if I tried saying it back to him, he would say, "No, you don't, I love you more!" It was a competition, a rigged game. In their negation of my own reciprocal feelings, those words felt empty. There was nothing to back them up.

I was tired of all the right words. I wanted a love and a life that didn't declare itself so much as demonstrated itself. I wanted to do the hard work of just being with myself and with another person attentively. I wanted to be as conscious as possible.

July Weekend

When I returned from the conference, David and I sat down to talk. I began to cry, which scared and surprised him. He tried to revoke his email, which, he said, he hadn't meant, he didn't actually think things were so bad. I realized that he couldn't hold the painful thoughts that were so beautifully expressed in his writing. They pained me as much as they did him, but I couldn't *not* hold them. And since I was holding them, I had to speak them.

Saying it all was harder than I would have predicted, given our past history of being so brutally honest with each other. But I had been lying to him for months, choosing to be dishonest about something that we would have talked about in the past. So I didn't know where to start. For his part, David was resistant to hearing any of it.

Our marriage was an impossible and increasingly damaging relationship kept together by the thick and rich history of love that we felt for each other. Neither of us could bear the thought of losing it. We were each other's salvation from our pasts. The smell of him, his sinewy forearms, his capacious hands and broad feet: these were the most familiar and loved things I had known for twenty-three years. We were each other's family. Cuddling up to him and the boys and the dog and the cat felt like burrowing into an animal den that was my home. My tail was tangled up with his, shit and blood and all.

Six years earlier, we had separated in anger. I'd adamantly insisted that I would thrive without him. The deep fear and insecurity that deluged me after the anger died down rocked my self-assurance. I couldn't bear how much I wanted to be back together with him. When he promised that he had changed, I was eager to believe it, so that I could return to him.

In those years of the second attempt, I tried to ignore all the ways that things were getting worse between us. I didn't even admit to myself that the affair had signaled the end. Until I read David's email and had to admit, since he had, that things were bad.

This time around, the decision came from a place that was different from my individual fear or resolve. I didn't know fully what I was doing, but I had come to trust the things I didn't really understand. I was taking definitive steps towards a truth that I did not want to see and could not fully comprehend.

It took many months. Often I felt unsure. I sometimes wondered how I knew if it was the right thing to do. How did I know that I wasn't running away again? I felt empty and listless. I missed the escape of the affair, but I didn't have the energy for that anymore.

David and I spent the entire summer and fall living together, drinking coffee in the early morning sun of the backyard and talking about the past and the future. After so many years of crisis and passion and volatility, we were calm, full of a quiet despair and dull terror. The boys adapted, without asking any questions, to us sleeping in separate rooms, though I was sure Liam sensed, on some level, what was happening. He came home from a friend's house once and said, "I'm glad our family is not like his. If you ever get divorced, I'll kill you."

Guilt and fear knotted my stomach; it made me feel nothing was worth wrecking his life like that. I would have stayed stuck, mired in panic, had Dr. O not suggested that maybe my son was not talking only about the marriage, but also about a split within me, the one that made me think that everything in my life was an either/or: either be the devoted perfect mother in the perfect family, or be the woman who sought escape from the chaos and confrontations of home in long work hours, in sex. As if Liam was actually saying, "How divorced you are within yourself is killing you."

It was. I felt myself to be dying as I struggled to maintain the stark division between what I didn't want to know — that a family could fall apart — and what I fantasized could still be true about me as an adult, as a wife, as a mother.

I still couldn't say clearly, "This is what I want." I kept second-guessing, and grasping at straws. What if I stopped thinking of David as my savior from my family, my past, myself? Could I stay with him then? I knew that he wanted to be my savior, as evidenced by his recurring dreams about rescuing me, or me and the children. We'd be stranded on a cliff, or swept by waves in a canoe, or threatened by a man with a weapon. He would risk his own life by running or swimming or fighting as hard as he could to stand between me and danger. When he told me about these dreams, I'd say he was sexist, and that he should stop fantasizing about rescuing a helpless woman. But his unconscious knew that my unconscious wanted him to get between me and a force within me that was bigger and more destructive than I could manage.

One July weekend, the four of us went to another family's farm. They were similar to us. The mother was the breadwinner, the father a writer, the children our kids' ages. But she was angrier maybe, and more trapped. When she drank she became disparaging about her husband's failings in front of their children. He laughed louder and got drunker to cover up her stream of abuse. David and I cringed to hear them, and were grateful for our gentleness towards each other, even though we were just pretending to still be a couple.

On Sunday, as we packed the kids and the dog into the car, our hosts smiled a congenial farewell. They stood in front of the farmhouse and waved us off in the setting sun. I was hit with a sickening pang of envy for this vision of what I no longer had: a happy nuclear family, biological parents standing next to each other with their offspring held close under protective arms. There were two images, then, of that family. One was the wretched couple bound by duty, financial constraint, habit, and dysfunctional repetition. The other was the beautiful lucky family in their rural idyll. A Rubin's vase: only one in focus at a time, the second negated by the force of the first; a parallax in which one disappears just as the other comes into view.

PART THREE

You Fucked Up My Life

Half of me knew that I needed to stay true to what I'm doing, which was separating from David so as to be able to stop splitting myself in two. I had lived with a crazy-making person for all these years. I couldn't bring myself to blame him, since I didn't think he did it on purpose, but he was so manipulative. The kids and I bent over backwards to make him feel affirmed. I made excuses for his behavior, believing in his exceptionalism. "Daddy's not like other people.... He's writing an important novel so that's why he is always scribbling in a notebook while you're in the playground.... He's going to grow vegetables for us so go help him dig.... He doesn't believe in authority so he doesn't have a job.... Daddy didn't come to pick you up because he lost track of time.... He's got a heightened sense of justice so he just yells at people in cars a lot.... You have to remind him to take you to soccer because he can't keep track of time."

Did I hear myself? Did I hear what I was doing to the kids, asking them to enable a man who should have been taking care of them? No, not really. I had been doing it for so long it felt like second nature.

Beautiful, fascinating David took up too much space and demanded an attention from me that was impossible to give. In response, I had non-confrontationally carved out secret spaces in which to dream and love and seek out what I needed to survive. Before our coupling there had been my family's own brand of manipulation and self-absorption. That situation, too, had demanded a sacrifice from me, a splitting in which I took the unwanted pieces to the woman who wanted them.

I had the chance now not to split myself. To try to inhabit fully my everyday life and my conscious mind and my active body. I had never done it. I'd liked the secrecy and the excitement and the self-division, but I was beginning to like the quieter calmer feeling that was becoming increasingly familiar in analysis. There wasn't much of that though. David kept breaking down in tears. Each time, it gouged both of our hearts.

Even though we were both in analysis, I didn't have much faith that David was learning about himself or about us. I also didn't feel that the unconscious murmurings and incoherent sentences that I spoke in Dr. O's office were tools enough for what we had to face. I looked online and found a couples counsellor who, I hoped, would be able to counsel us on how best to tell the children about our impending divorce. She was pale, with bright red lipstick and a navy blue suit. We sat in chairs in front of her, and I was calm and kind and jokey with him. After half an hour, she told us that she could see the love that there was between us, and that we should try to save our marriage. "Of course there is love," I said. "Tons of it. But that's not always a reason to stay together."

What she didn't see was that I was checked out of the marriage already. If I had still been engaged, I would have argued and attacked him in front of her. Instead I was friendly and distanced, because there was no need to hurt him further. I was furious, though, at her, that she had dared to pass a judgment on our two-decade-long marriage. And that she had gotten David's hopes up, because now he could use a professional's words against my own more inchoate ones. It was a trap: I should have performed the angry wife more, said brutal truths, stuck the knife in dramatically.

When he realized I wasn't going to do what that woman had suggested, David said to me, with a dull and fatalistic tone, "I wish I had never met you. You fucked up my life."

That hurt. To wish that was to erase all the years that we had lived and breathed each other. It negated our children, who we had sought so eagerly because our love was too much for just us. When our sons emerged, slippery and squawking, from my body into his waiting hands, we both felt the wonder and miracle of these living embodiments of our love. There could be, in my mind and heart, no undoing of this, no wishing it away. I regretted the lying I did and the pain we inflicted on each other, but not the being together.

I don't think he meant it. He was probably just lashing out with anything he could think of to hurt me. After all, I was the one doing the leaving, and his heart was just beginning to break, whereas mine had already started to heal. But the words resonated. How many men had I hurt enough that they wished they had never met me?

In our conversations, I was scrupulously careful with my words. I didn't want to say anything wrong, or be held accountable for any misrepresentation. The way the counselor had interpreted my demeanor had really scared me, and I felt watched and responsible for every step.

Dr. O noticed. "You're having trouble free-associating because everything you say has to be worth something?"

He was right. I didn't want to make any proclamations about my next steps. Didn't want to assert that I was wiser now, that I would no longer give myself away. I knew that I couldn't stop repeating my behaviors just by saying I was going to. I had to do it and then speak it.

In my fear, I was forgetting that analytic speaking was about bringing some other knowledge and awareness into words. It was not about proclamations. Dr. O and I never fought addiction or repetition by asserting that I would conquer it. We just kept speaking it, bringing it into increasingly obvious and clear language. It didn't feel like it was going to do anything, though. During that sad summer of separation, I felt hopeless.

It was a repetition of dark times in my past when I would wait for something horrible and have no words for it. Unable to speak it, I would act instead. But now I was looking for a way to hold words in suspension so that I wouldn't act destructively. Analysis was a space in which the words wouldn't dissolve in the face of darkness.

The waiting instead of acting was excruciating. I felt so helpless as I waited for some gesture or sign that would allow me to take the next step. It reminded me of when a dentist told me that I had to wait for my horrible mouth pain to localize so that she could isolate the affected tooth. That summer, I was waiting for the pain to tell me how to get at the root of the problem, so that I could resolve it.

I said to Dr. O, "How do I know that I'm not running away from analysis again, but this time by getting caught up in my divorce. I mean, why do I even want to separate from David?"

He said, "To find and understand part of your past, to bring the disparate parts of yourself together." It sounded too pat, too easy an answer. It also sounded true. I had been tangled up with David longer than I had been with my family of origin. But now I wanted to follow the lines from a part of myself that did not veer through him or them, threads that connected me with the person I was when I lay on the couch and spoke from my unconscious.

Heartbeat

Dr. O was going away on his August vacation, and I felt panicked that he would leave me in this state of fear and sadness.

I dreamt that I was pregnant. In the dream, I say to the midwife, "Don't you want to check for the heartbeat? I'm worried that something is wrong. Someone from outside my own body needs to verify whether the baby is alive."

When I told him, Dr. O said, "Need to know that the analysis is viable?"

That made me laugh, "So I need you to tell me if the analysis has got a heartbeat?"

But then I thought more about it and said seriously, "Maybe you don't even know."

He said, "I can hope."

The Third Term

David was never going to take the initiative to pack up and find a place of his own. We could have continued to live the way we were indefinitely if it had been up to him. Finally, in December

I put an end to this sad stasis by moving out of the house. I got a small apartment, which I kept tidy and sparse. The kids came on alternating weeks. We watched movies and read books. They wrestled the dog and each other on the couch. I felt really connected to them, like there was a line, a shiny thread, that stretched from me to each of them.

One afternoon David came over with Liam's forgotten soccer uniform. He was pretty manic, talking fast and loud. I offered him a coffee, since I was making myself one. Immediately he launched into a story about having stopped for coffee at A&W. To the server, he had made a joke about the Momma and the Poppa and the Teen burgers. She hadn't gotten it. And now his words were gulping and crescendoing between gales of hysterical laughter as he tried to tell us something about the extended family romance of the dead cow meat. The boys and I wanted in on the joke but didn't get it. When Liam caught my eye, I raised my eyebrows ever so slightly, but then we both immediately joined in David's laughter, careful to be with him, not with each other.

"I didn't think you ate fast food," I said.

"I don't! I've just become raw food vegan." He launched into a long explanation of plant proteins and enzyme absorption. Sebastian zoned out, while Liam eyes flitted back and forth between us. Minutes passed.

I blurted out, "David, enough already!" Was I allowed to still boss him around now that he was my ex? I wasn't sure, but continued, "Nutrition discussion is forbidden for the rest of the time that you're here." I saw Liam shoot me a look of relief.

"So," I said, "Did Sebastian tell you that he got into Northern High School?"

"Well, you know how I feel about education," David said to Sebastian.

Wait, what did Sebastian know? When had they talked about whatever it was that Princeton-educated David now thought of education? Was it in that string of emails that I saw sometimes in Sebastian's inbox, all still unread because "Mom, they're so long and incomprehensible"?

David did a slapstick impersonation of a school principal, which Liam gleefully joined, his hatred of his own principal fueling his antics. The four of us laughed and got as jittery as if we had all drunk a pot of coffee. Then David started to rant about the factory model of schooling, and how children should learn from roaming, foraging, and surviving in nature.

I finally told him that the boys had a lot of homework, despite his theories against it. The second he left, I felt the line go taut again, radiating out from me towards the two boys, true and straight. It was as if David had been sitting right in the middle of it, weighing it down. I saw how much space he took up, how crowded out I felt by his clamor for attention from me and from them. I also understood clearly how much the fantasy of the nuclear family weighed us all down, making our connections to each other so fraught and anxious. Each of us trying to perform the role that we felt was prescribed to us: father, mother, older son, younger son.

That line that I imagined wasn't the essential umbilical cord between mother and child. I knew better than to assume that there was anything natural or prescribed about a mother's love. It was a line that had been forged from my newly won ability to stay present, to not run away from the fear of failure or rejection that being a mother could elicit for me. I just stayed, right there, with whatever it was that was going on between us. Just like Dr. O and I stayed in analysis, every day.

I was building a wall, brick by brick, that held me, that kept the pieces from splitting off of me the way they used to when I was married. As I added bricks to the wall, I would trudge around the perimeter, mourning the things that were left out — the titillations and intrigues and seductions and spontaneous surprises. Even as I mourned though, I would still check to ensure that the walls were continuous. It was vital to protect what was inside the walls, even if it was less exciting than the fantasies.

I missed, of course, having the boys' father by my side so that we could laugh together at their jokes or reminisce about when they were little. I still dream about David often. In the dreams, we are always in an in-between space — an embankment, a shoreline, an airport, a train station. I hold him close to me, pressing my cheek against his and breathing in the smell of his skin. I murmur into his ear, "you know that I still love you, right? You know that I will always love you?" In the dream itself, I know that we are both committed to other people, and neither of us will ever cross the line of even a kiss. But the openheartedness of it — the absolute intimacy of how good it feels to hold him again — always left me bereft when I wake up.

In an earlier moment of my life, these dreams would have been a "ta da" moment, a revelation that showed me my true heart's desire on which I should act to live happily ever after. I would have used, I told Dr. O, summative reasoning:

(deep love) + (children's father) = stay married.

Saying the word "summative" in analysis — a word I had never used before — made me think of another administrative word that I had just heard used in a dean's meeting: "sectoral." I associated it with splitting up, cutting up.

Dr. O said, "Between the excitement of the summative and the pain of the sectoral, you are trying to find a balance."

"Yes. What's another 'S' word that speaks to that balance, to the place in the middle that is where I want to be? A third term?"

I thought for a while, and then said, "Sufficient."

Dr. O said, "Good enough."

One More Twist in the Spiral

I'd like to say that with the end of my marriage, with the new understanding I had about my own expectations and fears and desires, I was cured of my neurotic obsessions. But no, I continued to fuck things up. Not with my children, with whom I maintained that shiny line. But in other aspects, I was not cured. Yup… I almost ruined one more marriage.

I was lonely. I was horribly in debt from all the money I'd had to give David. I was horny. I wanted someone to care for me, protect me, and adore me. I knew by now that investing another person with all those abilities was only going to make me feel trapped and hateful towards him, but I still I indulged in one more fantasy.

There was a much older man, a family friend. He wanted to help. He loved talking to me. Having just had a health scare, he needed to feel loved and vital and attractive. I could give him that, in return for his attention. But this time I didn't have the fallback of my marriage. I couldn't say, like he did, "I could be a fantastic partner to you if I weren't married, but I am, and I have to be, because I can't help it, we have a history and a shared life and I am obligated to her."

Men who feared their wives, their parents, themselves: they had always been the ones who most turned me on. There was this conflict, this obligation and duty that kept them from being able to be with me, the one they really truly wanted. The hook was that it seemed like there was this whole beautiful thing just right around the corner, when they would be able to be with me fully. But there was never going to be that moment, because there was always going to be something that kept them with their heads up their asses. Maybe that's the way I wanted them anyway.

I yearned, and pined, and flirted. And then I got angry because I had made myself so vulnerable to him. I wanted to seduce him, and then drop him with indifferent beak. I even wore, when we went out to hear Bach's Cello Suites, a white sweater with feathers around the neck, like a swooping swan who would overpower him with her splendor. I felt so powerless and humiliated by my need that I got dangerously destructive, and didn't want to respect any lines.

I came close to ruining his marriage because of my continued insistence and presence. But I knew that I couldn't be with someone who would have to leave his wife to be with me. And I knew that I wouldn't put up for long with someone who wanted to take care of me. Most of all, I got so tired of hearing myself talking about it in analysis that it just petered out. My last daddy replacement. My last savior. My last attempt at seduction.

I was done.

Hue

In *Flowers for Algernon,* a book by Daniel Keyes that I read as a teenager, the main character, an intellectually disabled man, is given an experimental drug that raises his mental capacities.[55] He reads and loves a little blue copy of *Paradise Lost.* When the medication stops working, he relapses into his former state. He looks at the cover of the book, and knows that it gave him joy, but when he opens it, he can't understand it anymore.

Even though I've never reread it, this story has stayed with me. It begins with the limited language that the character has accessible to him, and moves from this unknowing to an increased awareness. He learns about himself, his relation to the world, his status and capacities, his sexual preferences, and his intellectual interests. And then he loses it again, and it seems like it was so tenuous to begin with, that foray into self-knowledge and connection with the world around him. What is actually changed by the experiment? Does he revert totally to his prior state, or has he been irrevocably changed? What is the status of "I," if it can be so radically erased or changed? If there are so many factors over which we do not have control?

What am I able to say about myself after the five years of psychoanalysis? In the slow process of bringing a demand, a symptom, an affect, into language, what emerged were not blinding moments of clarity, but rather what felt like a change in the hue of my memories and feelings. The many changes in my life over that period happened gradually, and it is only in retrospect that I can see the different coloration. But even beyond the discoveries or non-discoveries that I made, I experienced something else in that diurnal speaking. It was something about the form of telling stories, of listening to echoes and truths that could be heard if attended to with a free-floating attention.

Lacan says, "I don't discover the truth—I invent it."[56] We make our realities through the speaking of them. Psychoanalysis isn't, despite popular belief, about the uncovering of the past, but rather about the subjectification of one's own existence through language. Freud describes this as *"Wo Es war, soll Ich werden,"* which Lacan translates as, "Where it was, I must come into being."[57] Where before there had been desperate actions and unconscious motivations, now I was beginning to be able to speak my story into being. Where before I had imagined that there was an authority that dictated my desires, now I was putting into words the beliefs and assumptions that shaped my actions.

In *On Revolution,* Hannah Arendt talks about how our lives and memories can only be understood through narration. This involves a reworking and rethinking that situates events within a larger context and structure:

> Experiences and even the stories which grow out of what men do and endure, of happenings and events, sink back into the futility inherent in the living world and the living deed unless they are talked about over and over and over again. What saves the affairs of mortal men from their inherent futility is nothing but this incessant talk about them, which in its turn remains futile unless certain concepts, certain guideposts for future remembrance, and even for sheer reference, arise out of it.[58]

Where before I had told stories about my life, in analysis I became more able to see those stories as part of a larger framework of fear of abandonment, bicultural contradiction, internalized misogyny, sexual trauma, and class guilt.

In analysis, I spoke both the audible and the inaudible, and learned to listen to it. There was no shortcut for this. I couldn't have done it faster or better. I just had to do it. I learned how to speak only by speaking.

Towards the end of the analysis, before I knew it was the end, I wondered if what I had learned would endure beyond the scope of the sessions. When the narrator in *Flowers for Algernon* stops being able to speak himself as an intellectual, he stops being one. "I" is never irrevocable, it is always being shaped and transformed and injured by the sticky work of being human.

I hoped that when I terminated, I would continue to make time to think about things, analyze my dreams, or attend to the slips of the tongue and the moments of resistance that emerged in my daily life. But of course I haven't. I wake up with a half-remembered dream and instead of lying there trying to capture it, the way I did in analysis, I get up and do yoga, or make coffee, or walk the dog.

The repercussions of analysis have to be, I think, like the analysis itself. There, things flashed and disappeared. I half understood them, or I followed them for a bit and then dropped them, or I experienced them without full comprehension.

I learned a lot of things in analysis, and a lot changed. A lot didn't. A lot was lost, as was *Paradise Lost* for the character in *Flowers*. There are so many stories about which I gained knowledge, but there will always be another version, another way of bringing a truth into language.

Five Years In

We had often spent time together, me and David and the boys, Imre and his wife and their son. The two families took holidays together, and walked and cooked and drank beer and talked and talked. There's a Facebook photo of us two couples. It was taken at their going-away party. David is on one edge, Imre's wife on the other. Imre and I lean lightly with our arms around each other, slightly uncomfortable to be touching even though we are such old friends. My caption says, "We're going to miss you guys!" I didn't see them again after that, though they sent me their condolences when we divorced. They had tried to be friendly with David in the last few years of the marriage, but he had been argumentative and erratic, and they had chosen my side, urging me to leave him because they felt he was too much a burden on me.

When they divorced, Imre got in touch with me. She could have as well, but somehow the sides were chosen, and I became his confidante, not hers. We talked about how hard divorce was. Then we talked some more. Then we wrote to each other. Then, with a seriousness that took into account all the years of friendship and trust, we kissed. We've been together since. There wasn't much to say about it in analysis. There was no drama, no wrongdoing, no doubt or equivocation.

It is hard that I knew what Imre and his beautiful wife were like together. I loved who and how they were with each other. Sometimes the jealousy washes over me, to think of the laughter and adventures and intimacies they shared. But the relief and joy are greater:

That I didn't take him from her. That he didn't take me from David.

That he didn't love me while he was with her, but that he does now. That there is no triangle. That there is a direct line between us.

When we first got together and I told him about the men, I told him that I would never leave him for another. Imre said not to promise something I couldn't know. I said, "No, I can and do know this. I may end our relationship because I don't want to be with you anymore, but I will not run away from it, not escape into the fantasy of someone else."

My statement wasn't proclamative or prescriptive or performative; it was flatly declarative. It was spoken from my weariness, not from my determination. I was well and truly sick of how I had always cheated myself — of time, of energy, of concentration, of attention. I wasn't going to give it away anymore, because I knew, now, that I really wanted it for myself.

PART THREE

Personal Writing

David was the narrator of our lives. He kept notes of quirky things the kids had said, bits of dialogue, or random thoughts he had as he walked down city streets. When I told him what I thought about a film we'd seen or a book we'd both read, he'd write it up the next day as if it was his idea. I think he didn't even know what was his and what was mine. It was all blended together.

He almost wrote a lot of books, and I hope that he will one day finish one. But I couldn't read more than a paragraph or two at a time. They shared too much of our personal lives, and they were so crammed with argument and detail, every word planned for effect.

Now, here I am, writing a personal book full of details about our life together. It's like I took the space once I left him.

I tried to not write in this way. I believed, when I started writing this book, that I was still doing the "Too Much" project, but the personal kept coming into it. Then I tried to write more explicitly feminist stuff, intercalating my thoughts on subjectivity and gender politics and psychoanalysis with analyses of films and literature and contemporary events. I critiqued the self-improvement, self-awareness self-help rhetoric that I saw to be a product of neoliberalism's demands on us. But every time I wrote about it, I felt like I was being didactic or patronizing, like, "I have a more complicated and intellectual way of thinking about subjectivity, and I will point out how wrong people are in their beliefs about themselves." I felt especially uncomfortable when I tried to say something about sex and power, because I didn't want to come across as implying that other women were ignorant or deluded about their own empowerment or agency.

So I used "myself" as a case study. I followed the trajectory of a woman through a five-year psychoanalysis. It begins with her becoming aware of her pattern of giving pieces of herself away. It follows the repetitions of her fear and resistance as she seeks to not know things about herself. It ends with her trying to hold her multiple selves in all their contradictions. This beautiful woman, she was intelligent, educated, and trying her best, but she took herself too personally, believing that she could and should know herself and make the right choices. Through the practice of psychoanalysis, she came to understand that her self was made up of narratives that were larger and more amorphous than the ones that she thought she controlled. Narratives of gender, class, inheritance, sexual violence, and power shaped her actions, even as she thought she shaped them herself.

And I wrote it in the first person. In creating the "I" that speaks here, I have tried to not take myself personally. I don't want to see the act of writing as a gesture that discloses my most authentic self, because that would trigger my familiar hysterical demand for you to agree with me, to *like* me and what I say. Of course I still want your attention, and I will never be done with the clamoring voice that demands to be listened to and agreed with. But there are other voices that give shape to this book, voices that are more open, contradictory, and confused. Sometimes I write as a scholar, other times as a woman, a lover, a mother, a reader, an analysand, a girl. I know each of these roles is partial and not the one true voice of myself. In other words, I do not take any of them personally as I write them, since none of them are imbued with any particular authority that will persuade you as you read me.

Writing this book, though, has been as hard as the analysis itself. And it has taken as long. I wrote it in fragments, some just a line jotted down, others an academic essay, a diary entry, a long email, an accounting of the psychoanalytic session. Every time I settled down to edit, reorganize, conceptualize, I felt fear. Some days, I couldn't fight the underlying panic about the unviability of this book. My back seized up so that it hurt to sit. My gut churned as I drank coffee for courage. On the exterior, I looked the same as any of the other days. But there was turmoil just below the surface.

I'm still scared that this book will embarrass me, that I am harming my standing in the academic world. In the classroom and in my academic writing, I identify as an antihumanist, someone who questions unitary subjectivity and traditional interpretations of the human condition. I fear the confessional intimate mode of writing in this book will be seen as a reinscription of the subjectivity against which I argue.

When I write in a more academic voice, I attempt to protect myself, trying to prove points through research and quotation. That way, if my reader thinks I am wrong, I am at least at a remove from what I have written. What I see now is that my academic writing is actually fairly personal, all threaded through with implications and intonations and turns of phrase that beg to be admired.

This book is more vulnerable because I don't need to protect myself so much. I know that "myself" is a proliferation of selves who will say things that I don't want to say, do things I don't want to do, be hysterical, be cruel, be stupid, be vulnerable. So I have just written all the selves I could, and present them to you here as a study.

Don't take them, they're not yours. But they're not mine either. I just hold them all.

Georgian Bay

I rent a cottage for me, Imre, and friends to go write for a week. I want to once again see the pink Georgian Bay coastline and slanted trees. None of them have ever been to a house like this, so I am nervous that they will feel trapped and isolated on this remote island. The house itself is from the beginning of the twentieth century, and even though it is a grander version of the shack that David's family owns, it has the same wooden beams, creaky floors, and flimsy doors.

The second the boat docks I take off my shoes and don't put them on for the week. My feet shape themselves to the uneven surface and feel the different temperatures of the striated smooth rock as the sun passes over it. I inhale the sweet smell of the water as I float in its blue expanse. I step gingerly over the rock under which the rattlesnake rattles. My eyes are filled with the colors of the sunrise and sunset.

We cook elaborate meals and drink wine in the evenings. There are mosquitoes that make us scurry for cover as we try to roast marshmallows. And there are cockroaches ("Don't worry!" I say, "they're just pine bugs!") that we find in our suitcases, on our toothbrushes, and even in our beds. But I don't really notice if anyone minds. I am so happy to be living in that landscape again.

We write. Each of us claims a space on a porch or in an alcove or at a window. I get to the part in my writing where David and I separate. I walk out of the room where Imre and I have been sitting at parallel desks, and go find Catherine, my beautiful friend. I begin to tell her that I am scared to write, and burst into tears. A repository of so much of our history, from the early days at Duke when she would go on hikes with me and David, to the many visits of my boys with her boys, Catherine knows what it is to remember, and what it is to write. She cries with me. Then she gets up and moves all the furniture so that I can spread the pages out across the floor of the large living room. I sit on it with pens and scissors, and everyone steps carefully around the piles. And I see the shape of the whole book, and know what I will write.

I am in Georgian Bay, a place that holds many memories for me. I am there without David and all the chaos of what we were. I am doing the thing I most want to do — write this book — surrounded by people I love. As I write these lines, I know that they are good enough.

PART THREE

End of Analysis

It had been a year and a half since Imre and I got together. I still went to analysis five days a week, which was especially hard considering that Imre and I were in a commuting relationship. I was the director of Comparative Literature. David had not been able to maintain an apartment in Toronto and had moved to live with his aunt in the country, so I was a full-time mother.

Compared to what I had been doing for the previous years, my life felt so much easier. I wasn't running scared, juggling too many balls in the air. The analysis helped me focus on the things that needed to be spoken and acknowledged. I could slow down enough to feel what I had shut out before. I was sad that David wasn't in the boys' lives, but confident that I would not fail them. I knew that what Sebastian and Liam needed was for me to be there, to not avoid anything, no matter how painful. So whether I had to set boundaries around substance use, or stay up late talking about puberty or video games or their father, I leaned into each conversation, trying my hardest to not take personally their emotions or their defiance.

Imre and I were going to run a three-week residency at the Banff Centre, and I went ahead with the plans for it before deciding what I was going to do about the analysis. At first I figured I would just pay for the three weeks, which would be very expensive, but at least I would be getting free room and board during that time. I thought about asking Dr. O if he would do analysis over the phone, though I couldn't imagine what that would feel like. Considering that he wrote his bills to me on thick stationery with a fountain pen, he seemed to be too traditional for that.

A couple of months before we were to go, I realized what my plan was. I was going to end the analysis. I picked a date, exactly 5 years and 5 days after I had started, and told Dr. O that would be my final day. I didn't even know that I was going to until I heard myself calmly say it. He didn't respond.

A few days later, I alluded to the date again. He said something like, "Yes, you mentioned that date." We carried on talking about something else.

The third time I brought it up, he pushed back, and said, "How do you know you're not hitting up against something, and that this is another form of resistance? Are you ending in order to run away?"

A year earlier, this would have made my gut churn with anxiety. But this time, I just said, "No, I can tell that it's not resistance. It doesn't have a prickle to it. I love what we do here — I'm not running away from it. It's just that I know it's time to end it. I know it not in an intuitive, instinctual, quiver in my gut way, but in my head and heart and quiet bones."

He said, "Mmm."

For the next six weeks, we carried on the analysis with no movement towards "wrapping it up", whatever that would have meant. I continued to recount my dreams, many of which were about walking, either alone or with him, on a shore or along a cliff. The ocean didn't hold the same dread as it had in the earlier dreams. We looked down or across at it, and continued to walk on the path.

In those last days, I kept forgetting his name. It's not like I ever had it on the tip of my tongue anyway, and I usually called him "my shrink" when I talked about him to others. But this was different. I really had no idea what his name was, and would confuse it with other names. During much of the analysis, I had feared that he held parts of me in some secret place within him. Now I felt like we were both nobody, that the particularities of each of us as individuals were irrelevant. I would lie on the couch trying to remember his name and thinking that if I ever wrote a book about anything that had emerged during the analysis, I would dedicate it to "whoever that was that sat behind the couch."

And then it was Friday, May 16, 2015. I lay on the couch and had a sharp clear image of a wide meadow in the sunlight. Dr. O and I walked out of a dark cool wood, and stood at the edge of the meadow making out a faint path that wound through the tall grasses. He stayed on the edge, and I began to walk along the path towards the middle of the meadow, feeling the sun on my face and the breeze on my skin.

He said, "It makes me think of that Bobby Burns poem that says something about "when a body meets a body walking in the rye."[59]

I said I liked that, that it's not nobody and it's not somebody; it just two impersonal bodies that come into contact and do something with each other.

We both thought a bit. He said that the catcher in the rye is the one who keeps the children from falling off the cliff.

I remembered the Pied Piper, and said, "This image is the opposite. Instead of leading them off the edge of the cliff, the catcher in the rye contains them, keeps the different pieces from flying off. You have been my catcher. Now I am stepping into the rye. I'll be my own catcher."

Then I said that I wished somehow that I had his blessing to end the analysis. Or maybe that I needed to give him mine. "Well," he said, "it was your decision to end the analysis."

"Yes it was."

He said, "What better blessing than that?"

We fell silent together, a silence that we both listened to, knowing that there would be no more words between us. And then, as opposed to what he had said every day for five years — "And that's our time for today" — he said, "And that's our time to end." I stood up and walked to the door, and turned around to look at him. I think that I thought that I should thank him, that I would regret it forever if I didn't.

He was standing slightly stooped, with his head turned a bit to one side. I looked directly into his eyes and smiled seriously, and he nodded in acknowledgment. And then.... I don't remember what I did. I don't know if I said "Thank you" or if I just turned and walked out the door.

It doesn't matter. It had been a long and painful conversation that had shaped us in relation to each other. In that room, we had held each other accountable for our words and actions. We attended to whatever was brought into words. And we held it. Everything that had happened between us was not going to be summed up in those words.

There was no one to thank.

Endnotes

1 Jacques Lacan, *Écrits: A Selection,* trans. Alan Sheridan (New York, Norton, 1966), 127.
2 Jacques Lacan, quoted in Bruce Fink, *Fundamental of Psychoanalytic Technique: A Lacanian Approach for Practitioners* (New York: W.W. Norton, 2007), 11.
3 Bhanu Kapil, *The Vertical Interrogation of Strangers* (Berkeley: Kelsey Street Press, 2001), 9.
4 Alain Badiou, *Ethics: An Essay on the Understanding of Evil,* trans. Peter Hallward (New York: Verso, 2012), 55.
5 D.W. Winnicott, *Transitional Objects and Transitional Phenomena through Paediatrics to Psycho-analysis: Collected Papers* (New York: Basic Books, 1951), 11.
6 Walter Benjamin, "The Work of Art in the Age of Mechanical Reproduction," in *Illuminations: Essays and Reflections,* trans. Harry Zohn, ed. Hannah Arendt (New York: Schocken Books, 2007), 217–51, at 237.
7 Sigmund Freud, "A Case of Hysteria (1905)," in *The Standard Edition of the Complete Psychological Works of Sigmund Freud, Volume VII (1901–1905): A Case of Hysteria, Three Essays on Sexuality and Other Works,* ed. and trans. James Strachey with Anna Freud (London: The Hogarth Press and the Institute of Psychoanalysis, 1953), 1–122, at 76–77.
8 Sigmund Freud, "Three Essays on the Theory of Sexuality (1905)," in *The Standard Edition of the Complete Psychological Works of Sigmund Freud, vol. VII (1901–1905): A Case of Hysteria, Three Essays on Sexuality and Other Works,* ed. and trans. James Strachey with Anna Freud (London: The Hogarth Press and the Institute of Psychoanalysis, 1953), 123–230, at 185.
9 Walter Benjamin, "The Image of Proust," in *Illuminations: Essays and Reflections,* trans. Harry Zohn, ed. Hannah Arendt (New York: Schocken Books, 1969), 201–15, at 207.
10 Eve Kosofsky Sedgwick, "Is the Rectum Straight? Identification and Identity in The Wings of the Dove," in *Tendencies* (London: Duke University Press, 1993), 73–103.

11 Henry James, *The Wings of the Dove* (London: Penguin, 1986), 57, quoted in Sedgwick, "Is the Rectum Straight?" 82.
12 Ibid., 81.
13 Jacques Lacan, *The Seminar of Jacques Lacan, Book XI: The Four Fundamental Concepts of Psychoanalysis,* ed. Jacques-Alain Miller, trans. Alan Sheridan (New York: W.W. Norton, 1998), 230.
14 Jacques Lacan, *The Seminar of Jacques Lacan, Book III: The Psychoses 1955-56,* ed. Jacques-Alain Miller, trans. Russell Grigg (London: Routledge, 1993), 170-75.
15 Wisława Szymborska, "Autotomy," in *Nothing Twice: Selected Poems,* ed. and trans. Stanisław Barańczak and Claire Cavanaugh (Warsaw: Wydawnictwo Literackie, 1997), 157.
16 Sigmund Freud, "Neurosis and Psychosis," in *The Standard Edition of the Complete Psychological Works of Sigmund Freud, Volume XIX (1923-1925): The Ego and the Id and Other Works,* ed. and trans. James Strachey with Anna Freud (London: The Hogarth Press and the Institute of Psychoanalysis, 1955), 147-54; 151-52.
17 Sigmund Freud, "Observations on Transference-Love (Further Recommendations on the Technique of Psycho-Analysis III)," in *The Standard Edition of the Complete Psychological Works of Sigmund Freud, Volume XII (1911-1913): The Case of Schreber, Papers on Technique, and Other Works,* ed. and trans. James Strachey with Anna Freud (London: The Hogarth Press and the Institute of Psychoanalysis, 1955), 159-71.
18 Ibid., 170.
19 Ursula Le Guin, *The Dispossessed: An Ambiguous Utopia* (New York: PerfectBound, 2002), 468
20 Paul de Man, "The Rhetoric of Temporality," in *Blindness and Insight: Essays in the Rhetoric of Contemporary Criticism* (London: Routledge, 1989), 187-228, at 207.
21 Dylan Thomas, letter to Henry Treece, 23 March 1938, in *The Selected Letters of Dylan Thomas,* ed. Constantine FitzGibbon (London: Dent, 1966), 190-91.
22 D.W. Winnicott, "The Theory of the Parent-Infant Relationship," in *The Maturational Processes and the Facilitating Environment* (New York: International Universities Press, 1965), 37-55.
23 Rosalind Gill, "Critical Respect: The Difficulties and Dilemmas of Agency and 'Choice' for Feminism," *European Journal of Women's Studies* 14, no. 1 (2007): 69-80, at 76.
24 Czesław Miłosz, "Ars Poetica?" trans. Czesław Miłosz and Lillian Vallee, *Poetry Foundation,* https://www.poetryfoundation.org/poems/49455/ars-poetica-56d22b8f31558.
25 Jacques Rancière, *The Ignorant Schoolmaster: Five Lessons in Intellectual Emancipation,* trans. Kristin Ross (Stanford: Stanford University Press, 1999).
26 Allison Bechdel, *Are You My Mother? A Comic Drama* (Boston: Houghton Mifflin Harcourt, 2012), quoting D.W. Winnicott, "The Use of An Object."

27 Stephin Merritt/Magnetic Fields, "Absolutely Cuckoo," *69 Love Songs* (Polar West Studios, 1999).
28 W.B. Yeats, "Leda and the Swan," in *The Collected Poems of W.B. Yeats*, ed. Richard J. Finnera (New York: Simon & Schuster, 1996), 214.
29 Camille Paglia, *Sexual Personae: Art and Decadence from Nefertiti to Emily Dickinson* (New Haven: Yale University Press, 2001), 268.
30 Marcel Proust, *In Search of Lost Time, vol. 1: Swann's Way*, trans. C.K. Scott Moncrieff and Terence Kilmartin, rev. D.J. Enright (New York: The Modern Library, 1992), 49–50.
31 Theodor Adorno, *Minima Moralia: Reflections on a Damaged Life*, trans. E.F.N. Jephcott (London: Verso: 2006), 171.
32 Thomas Mann, *The Magic Mountain*, trans. John E. Woods (New York: Alfred A. Knopf, 1995), xxxvi.
33 Fredric Jameson, *The Modernist Papers* (London: Verso, 2007), 63.
34 Alain Badiou, *Handbook of Inaesthetics*, trans. Alberto Toscano (Stanford: Stanford University Press, 2005), 1.
35 Fredric Jameson, *The Political Unconscious: Narrative as a Socially Symbolic Act* (Ithaca: Cornell University Press, 1981), 9.
36 Jacques Lacan, *The Seminar of Jacques Lacan, Book I: Freud's Papers on Technique 1953–1954*, ed. Jacques-Alain Miller, trans. John Forrester (New York: W.W. Norton, 1991), 278.
37 Ibid.
38 Ibid.
39 Slavoj Žižek, *Enjoy Your Symptom: Jacques Lacan in Hollywood and Out* (New York: Routledge, 1992), 104..
40 Sophie De Mijolla-Mellor. "Acting Out/Acting In," *Encyclopedia.com*, https://www.encyclopedia.com/psychology/dictionaries-thesauruses-pictures-and-press-releases/acting-outacting.
41 Ibid.
42 Philip Roth, *Portnoy's Complaint* (New York: Random House, 1969), 271.
43 Jacques Lacan, "Introduction to Jean Hyppolite's Commentary on Freud's 'Verneinung,'" in *Écrits: The First Complete Edition in English*, trans. Bruce Fink (New York: W.W. Norton, 2005), 308–17, at 317n4.
44 Lacan, *The Four Fundamental Concepts of Psychoanalysis*, 88.
45 Jacques Lacan, *The Seminar of Jacques Lacan, Book VII: The Ethics of Psychoanalysis 1959–1960*, ed. Jacques-Alain Miller, trans. Dennis Porter (New York: W.W. Norton, 1997), 135.
46 Sigmund Freud, "Two Encyclopaedia Articles: (A) Psycho-Analysis," in *The Standard Edition of the Complete Psychological Works of Sigmund Freud, Volume XVIII (1920–1922): Beyond the Pleasure Principle, Group Psychology and Other Works*, ed. and trans. James Strachey with Anna Freud (London: The Hogarth Press and the Institute of Psychoanalysis, 1955), 235–54, at 239.
47 Courtney Barnett, "Pedestrian at Best," *Sometimes I Sit and Think, And Sometimes I Just Sit* (Head Gap Studio, 2015).

48 Philip Pullman, *The Golden Compass* (New York: Alfred A. Knopf, 2002), 214.
49 See Lacan, *The Ethics of Psychoanalysis*, 319–24.
50 Lee Priestly, *The Two Too Twins* (Boston: Whitman, 1966).
51 See Jacques Lacan's discussion of the "four discourses" in *The Seminar of Jacques Lacan, Book XVII: The Other Side of Psychoanalysis,* trans. Russell Grigg (New York: W.W. Norton, 2006).
52 Marcel Proust, *In Search of Lost Time, vol. 2: Within a Budding Grove,* ed. D.J. Enright, trans. C.K. Scott Moncrieff (New York: Modern Library, 1998), 357.
53 Lacan, *The Other Side of Psychoanalysis,* 51.
54 Badiou, *Ethics,* 47.
55 Daniel Keyes, *Flowers for Algernon* (New York: Harcourt, Brace & World, 1966).
56 Jacques Lacan, quoted in Fink, *Fundamentals of Psychoanalytic Technique,* 33.
57 Jacques Lacan, "The Instance of the Letter in the Unconscious," in *Écrits: A Selection,* 524.
58 Hannah Arendt, *On Revolution* (London: Penguin, 1990), 220.
59 Robert Burns, "Comin' Thro' the Rye," in *Selected Poems,* intro. Andrew Lang (London: K. Paul, Trench, Trübner, 1891), 201.

Bibliography

Adorno, Theodor. *Minima Moralia: Reflections on a Damaged Life.* Translated by E.F.N. Jephcott. London: Verso: 2006.
Arendt, Hannah. *On Revolution.* London: Penguin, 1990.
Badiou, Alain. *Ethics: An Essay on the Understanding of Evil.* Translated by Peter Hallward. New York: Verso, 2012.
———. *Handbook of Inaesthetics.* Translated by Alberto Toscano. Stanford: Stanford University Press, 2005.
Barnett, Courtney. "Pedestrian at Best," *Sometimes I Sit and Think, And Sometimes I Just Sit.* Head Gap Studio, 2015.
Bechdel, Allison. *Are You My Mother? A Comic Drama.* Boston: Houghton Mifflin Harcourt, 2012.
Benjamin, Walter. "The Image of Proust." In *Illuminations: Essays and Reflections,* translated by Harry Zohn, edited by Hannah Arendt, 201–15. New York: Schocken Books, 1969.
———. "The Work of Art in the Age of Mechanical Reproduction." In *Illuminations: Essays and Reflections,* translated by Harry Zohn, edited by Hannah Arendt, 217–51. New York: Schocken Books, 2007.
Burns, Robert. *Selected Poems.* Introduction by Andrew Lang. London: K. Paul, Trench, Trübner, 1891.
de Man, Paul. "The Rhetoric of Temporality." In *Blindness and Insight: Essays in the Rhetoric of Contemporary Criticism,* 187–228. London: Routledge, 1989.
De Mijolla-Mellor, Sophie. "Acting Out/Acting In." *Encyclopedia.com.* https://www.encyclopedia.com/psychology/

dictionaries-thesauruses-pictures-and-press-releases/
acting-outacting.

Fink, Bruce. *Fundamental of Psychoanalytic Technique: A Lacanian Approach for Practitioners*. New York: W.W. Norton, 2007.

Freud, Sigmund. "A Case of Hysteria (1905)." In *The Standard Edition of the Complete Psychological Works of Sigmund Freud, Volume VII (1901–1905): A Case of Hysteria, Three Essays on Sexuality and Other Works*, edited and translated by James Strachey with Anna Freud, 1–122. London: The Hogarth Press and the Institute of Psychoanalysis, 1953.

———. "Observations on Transference-Love (Further Recommendations on the Technique of Psycho-Analysis III)." In *The Standard Edition of the Complete Psychological Works of Sigmund Freud, Volume XII (1911–1913): The Case of Schreber, Papers on Technique, and Other Works*, edited and translated by James Strachey with Anna Freud, 159–71. London: The Hogarth Press and the Institute of Psychoanalysis, 1955.

———. "Three Essays on the Theory of Sexuality (1905)." In *The Standard Edition of the Complete Psychological Works of Sigmund Freud, vol. VII (1901–1905): A Case of Hysteria, Three Essays on Sexuality and Other Works*, edited and translated by James Strachey with Anna Freud, 123–230. London: The Hogarth Press and the Institute of Psychoanalysis, 1953.

———. "Two Encyclopaedia Articles: (A) Psycho-Analysis." In *The Standard Edition of the Complete Psychological Works of Sigmund Freud, Volume XVIII (1920–1922): Beyond the Pleasure Principle, Group Psychology and Other Works*, edited and translated by James Strachey with Anna Freud, 235–54. London: The Hogarth Press and the Institute of Psychoanalysis, 1955.

Gill, Rosalind. "Critical Respect: The Difficulties and Dilemmas of Agency and 'Choice' for Feminism." *European Journal of Women's Studies* 14, no. 1. (2007): 69–80. DOI: 10.1177/1350506807072318.

James, Henry. *The Wings of the Dove*. London: Penguin, 1986.

Jameson, Fredric. *The Modernist Papers*. London: Verso, 2007.

———. *The Political Unconscious: Narrative as a Socially Symbolic Act*. Ithaca: Cornell University Press, 1981.

Kapil, Bhanu. *The Vertical Interrogation of Strangers*. Berkeley: Kelsey Street Press, 2001.

Keyes, Daniel. *Flowers for Algernon*. New York: Harcourt, Brace & World, 1966.

Kosofsky Sedgwick, Eve. "Is the Rectum Straight? Identification and Identity in The Wings of the Dove." In *Tendencies*, 73–103. London: Duke University Press, 1993.

Lacan, Jacques. *Écrits: A Selection*. Translated by Alan Sheridan. New York, Norton, 1966.

———. "Introduction to Jean Hyppolite's Commentary on Freud's 'Verneinung.'" In *Écrits: The First Complete Edition in English*, translated by Bruce Fink, 308–17. New York: W.W. Norton, 2005.

———. *The Seminar of Jacques Lacan, Book I: Freud's Papers on Technique 1953–1954*. Edited by Jacques-Alain Miller, translated by John Forrester. New York: W.W. Norton, 1991.

———. *The Seminar of Jacques Lacan, Book III: The Psychoses 1955–56*. Edited by Jacques-Alain Miller, translated by Russell Grigg. London: Routledge, 1993.

———. *The Seminar of Jacques Lacan, Book VII: The Ethics of Psychoanalysis 1959–1960*. Edited by Jacques-Alain Miller, translated by Dennis Porter. New York: W.W. Norton, 1997.

———. *The Seminar of Jacques Lacan, Book XI: The Four Fundamental Concepts of Psychoanalysis*. Edited by Jacques-Alain Miller, translated by Alan Sheridan. New York: W.W. Norton, 1998.

———. *The Seminar of Jacques Lacan, Book XVII: The Other Side of Psychoanalysis*. Translated by Russell Grigg. New York: W.W. Norton, 2006.

Le Guin, Ursula. *The Dispossessed: An Ambiguous Utopia*. New York: PerfectBound, 2002.

Mann, Thomas. *The Magic Mountain*. Translated by John E. Woods. New York: Alfred A. Knopf, 1995.

Miłosz, Czesław. "Ars Poetica?" Translated by Czesław Miłosz and Lillian Vallee. *Poetry Foundation.* https://www.poetryfoundation.org/poems/49455/ars-poetica-56d22b8f31558

Merritt, Stephin/Magnetic Fields. "Absolutely Cuckoo," *69 Love Songs.* Polar West Studios, 1999.

Paglia, Camille. *Sexual Personae: Art and Decadence from Nefertiti to Emily Dickinson.* New Haven: Yale University Press, 2001.

Priestly, Lee. *The Two Too Twins.* Boston: Whitman, 1966.

Proust, Marcel. *In Search of Lost Time, Vol. 1: Swann's Way.* Translated by C.K. Scott Moncrieff and Terence Kilmartin, revised by D.J. Enright. New York: The Modern Library, 1992.

———. *In Search of Lost Time, Vol. 2: Within a Budding Grove.* Edited by D.J. Enright, translated by C.K. Scott Moncrieff. New York: Modern Library, 1998.

Pullman, Philip. *The Golden Compass.* New York: Alfred A. Knopf, 2002.

Rancière, Jacques. *The Ignorant Schoolmaster: Five Lessons in Intellectual Emancipation.* Translated by Kristin Ross. Stanford: Stanford University Press, 1999.

Roth, Philip. *Portnoy's Complaint.* New York: Random House, 1969.

Szymborska, Wisława. *Nothing Twice: Selected Poems.* Edited and translated by Stanisław Barańczak and Claire Cavanaugh. Warsaw: Wydawnictwo Literackie, 1997.

Thomas, Dylan. *The Selected Letters of Dylan Thomas.* Edited by Constantine FitzGibbon. London: Dent, 1966.

Winnicott, D.W. "The Theory of the Parent-Infant Relationship." In *The Maturational Processes and the Facilitating Environment,* 37–55. New York: International Universities Press, 1965.

———. *Transitional Objects and Transitional Phenomena through Paediatrics to Psycho-analysis: Collected Papers.* New York: Basic Books, 1951.

Yeats, W.B. *The Collected Poems of W.B. Yeats.* Edited by Richard J. Finnera. New York: Simon & Schuster, 1996.

Žižek, Slavoj. *Enjoy Your Symptom: Jacques Lacan in Hollywood and Out.* New York: Routledge, 1992.